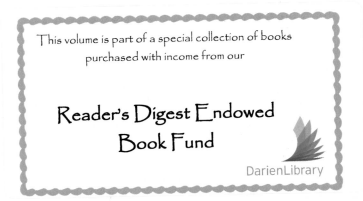

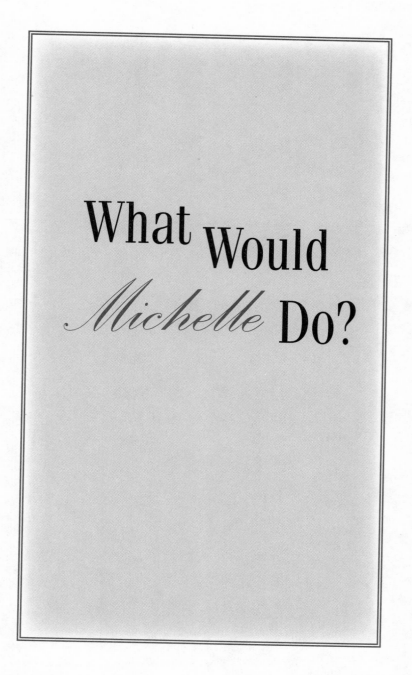

What Would Would Michelle Do?

What Would

Would

Michelle Do?

A Modern-Day Guide to
Living with Substance and Style

Allison Samuels

GOTHAM BOOKS

GOTHAM BOOKS
Published by Penguin Group (USA) Inc.
375 Hudson Street, New York, New York 10014, U.S.A.
Penguin Group (Canada), 90 Eglinton Avenue East, Suite 700, Toronto, Ontario
M4P 2Y3, Canada (a division of Pearson Penguin Canada Inc.); Penguin Books
Ltd, 80 Strand, London WC2R 0RL, England; Penguin Ireland, 25 St Stephen's
Green, Dublin 2, Ireland (a division of Penguin Books Ltd); Penguin Group
(Australia), 250 Camberwell Road, Camberwell, Victoria 3124, Australia (a
division of Pearson Australia Group Pty Ltd); Penguin Books India Pvt Ltd, 11
Community Centre, Panchsheel Park, New Delhi—110 017, India; Penguin Group
(NZ), 67 Apollo Drive, Rosedale, Auckland 0632, New Zealand (a division of
Pearson New Zealand Ltd); Penguin Books (South Africa) (Pty) Ltd, 24 Sturdee
Avenue, Rosebank, Johannesburg 2196, South Africa

Penguin Books Ltd, Registered Offices: 80 Strand, London WC2R 0RL, England

Published by Gotham Books, a member of Penguin Group (USA) Inc.

First printing, April 2012
10 9 8 7 6 5 4 3 2 1

LIBRARY OF CONGRESS CATALOGING-IN-PUBLICATION DATA
Samuels, Allison.
    What would Michelle do? : a modern-day guide to living with substance and
style / Allison Samuels.
        p. cm.
    ISBN 978-1-59240-708-8 (hbk.)
    1. Women—Conduct of life. 2. Self-realization in women. 3. Obama, Michelle,
1964-   —Influence. I. Title.
    BJ1610.S345 2012
    646.70082—dc23   2011048768

All illustrations courtesy of Megan Hess

Printed in the United States of America
Set in Bell MT Std
Designed by Spring Hoteling

To my mother, Classie West, for her unconditional love and support, and for passing on a love of style, culture, and all things Jackie, Audrey, and Michelle

Contents

Introduction

*H*owever does she do it?

How does First Lady Michelle Obama juggle the many hats she must don daily without ever breaking the proverbial sweat that would surely dismantle her perfectly coiffed bob?

Whether hula hooping in the front yard of the White House alongside schoolkids or wowing foreign dignitaries at an official state dinner, Michelle Obama approaches whatever situation she's in with a steely calm and humble grace remarkably reminiscent of many of the iconic women who've come before her. This has ushered her into an elite club of women who need only be referenced by their first name to garner instant recognition and unyielding reverence. As vivid images of Michelle surface on television, on popular Web sites, and in fashion magazines, names like Grace, Audrey, and Jackie spring to mind. Michelle has joined the ranks of these fabulous women who all used their signature kitten-heel pumps to walk right into our hearts, leaving an indelible mark.

Much has been and certainly will continue to be written

about the First African-American FLOTUS (First Lady of the United States). In a valiant effort to dictate history, many will attempt to explain the complicated inner workings of this classy, cultured, yet incredibly approachable woman. With her perfectly poised posture, gracious charm, and infectious vitality, Michelle has mesmerized the world since her arrival in the public spotlight back in 2006. Not since Jackie O nearly a quarter of a century ago has a First Lady held our attention so intently, her every move analyzed and her every word remembered.

What exactly is so special about Michelle?

Maybe it's her rise from a working-class background to the hallowed halls of the Ivy League and on to the White House that resonates so soundly with the masses. Maybe it's the easy way she seems to connect with virtually everyone around her, appearing never to lose touch or her down-home charm. Maybe it's the loving way she supports her husband without appearing the least bit subservient or surrendered. Or maybe it's all of the above.

In this book, you'll discover a myriad of ways to channel your own inner Michelle using many of her everyday, lifelong rules of thumb. Ready, willing, and able to lovingly lead you over and around life's many twists and turns, she's the über-stylish and ultra-hip role model so unflappable that she's able to converse as effortlessly with Beyoncé, the queen of pop, as she does with Kate Middleton, the future queen of England.

Culled from her personal experience, these are the best ways to develop and maintain Michelle's cool self-assurance in all facets of your life. Following Michelle's guidelines for personal growth and satisfaction, you'll be able to determine and develop your own true passions. Michelle's own storied journey will offer clues on how to find and obtain a rich destiny for yourself that doesn't depend on snagging Dwyane Wade or George Clooney. Tidbits large and small from the First Lady's well-organized and thoughtfully planned life will offer innovative ways to create a fun and loving bond with your children and do the very same with your own parents. In an age where temper tantrums and physical confrontations with foes and friends alike are rewarded with television contracts, the First Lady's very modern yet very thoughtful and courteous way of life can be just the reminder you need to understand what truly being a lady entails. So, whether you're seeking a more thorough understanding of your life's true passions or want assistance in choosing a well-rounded, supportive inner circle, Michelle's well-trodden path will lead the way.

Michelle's life also offers insight into obtaining those perfectly toned but feminine arms, that sinewy frame, and a partner who will still give us love-struck gazes after many years of marriage, just like Barack. Details of the Obamas' long love affair will provide commonsense pointers on how to secure a love of your own that will last a lifetime.

Finally, this book will pull no punches because, quite frankly, when all is said and done, Michelle wouldn't have it any other way. She'd be the first to acknowledge how her strong family ties and top-notch education coupled with the hand of fate have changed and enhanced her life in ways most women can't imagine for their own.

But in true Michelle style, after admitting the extraordinary existence she's been privileged to lead, she'd no doubt offer you the same advice she gives recent college graduates and women from all walks of life:

"Something amazing is out there waiting for you, but you won't ever find it if you don't ever look."

Chapter One
Find Your Seat and Take It

You know every time somebody told me, No, you can't do that, I pushed past their doubts and I took my seat at the table.

—MO

Without fail the first observation expressed by those who've had the pleasure of being graced with Michelle Obama's presence through the years is that she possesses a remarkable sense of self. Though it's difficult to fully comprehend for those of us not so fortunate, Michelle Obama appears to have come into the world completely aware of and quite comfortable with exactly who she was born to be.

Self-awareness is a trait that Michelle obtained early on and continues to display prominently to this day. Though it may seem otherwise, she actually wasn't born with it. While some of her no-nonsense attitude and can-do philosophy is indeed instinctive, a great deal of what makes Michelle who she is was cultivated, nurtured, and learned. These were things that were taught to her by parents who loved her, mentors she sought out, and the reality of circumstances she couldn't change but was committed to overcoming, even if it meant observing others and teaching herself. Supreme confidence and unshakable self-esteem have been constant mainstays in the First Lady's life. So it should go without saying that in order to channel any part of Michelle, you'll have to find yourself first.

Her Roots

Michelle LaVaughn Robinson's keen awareness began one January morning in 1964, the year she was born into an all-American family on the South Side of Chicago. She joined older brother Craig, homemaker mother Marian, and father Fraser Robinson in a modest, immaculately kept one-bedroom apartment in a working-class African-American community. Young Michelle thrived in her secure surroundings, which heaped loads of love, acceptance, and support on both children.

From all accounts, the Robinsons encouraged their daughter to explore absolutely everything around her as soon as she was old enough to grasp what everything meant. This was Marian and Fraser's way of instantly conveying to their children the deep and never-ending connection between great knowledge and unwavering confidence. The Robinsons left little to chance. They were proud parents of two African-American children born during the middle of the civil rights movement. Additional instructions weren't just needed—they were required.

So the Robinsons took it a step further and instilled a no-nonsense attitude, strong work ethic, and positive mind-set Michelle could rely on to succeed.

My parents always said: "Don't tell us what you can't do."

—MO

Like a good soldier, Michelle latched on to these early lessons and held on for dear life. She ultimately believed that her family's repeated nuggets of common sense and wisdom would one day enable her to float easily from one arena of life into another without so much as a thought. And she was right.

At the mere age of thirteen, Michelle was chosen to attend a more racially diverse junior high school on the other side of town. The change would require her to abandon the warm comfort of her family, neighborhood, and close friends, taking several buses to travel to a strange new world. Did Michelle hesitate to take advantage of this opportunity? Absolutely not! She was completely undaunted by the new challenge.

"We were looking for the top kids we could find," said Charles Mingo, then an assistant principal at Whitney M. Young Magnet High School, the school Michelle attended. "Her parents knew that even at that age, she was mature and ambitious and could handle the transition, though she'd know virtually no one."

Serious, sensible, and straightforward, Michelle sailed through the first year at her new school without so much as a hitch, leaving her fellow students and teachers in awe of her quiet, determined demeanor and her crystal-clear point of view.

Rule of Thumb No. 1: Remember My Name

Even as a young girl with little exposure to the massive world around her, Michelle left an indelible impression on

everyone she came into contact with. Many of her peers remember her as a "respectable young lady, always perfectly
groomed, and exceptionally well behaved." Her teachers instantly recall encounters with the then-teenage girl as if it
were yesterday. One legendary tale recounts Michelle challenging her typing teacher on a grade she received and
thought unfair. Michelle's mother, Marian, recalls how Michelle received a B on an assignment she felt sure she deserved an A for. She met with the teacher and explained in
detail each reason why she felt her paper had been penalized
unfairly on certain points. "We taught our children not to
challenge authority but to stand up for what they believed
in," Marian Robinson explains. That's exactly what Michelle did. She was so dogmatic and unrelenting in her pro-
tests that she finally did receive the A she knew she deserved.
We often focus on making a great first impression, but the
moral of this story is to always look great, handle yourself
well, and stand up for what you believe is right. These actions will prove life affirming for you and unforgettable to
others.

Stand Out in a Crowded World

Confidence is the best friend a woman can have. It should be
more coveted than a pair of pearls, diamonds, or even a floor-
length fur. Confidence like Michelle's demands and com-
mands attention from everyone around you, which only helps
your self-esteem grow.

Projecting a confident attitude shows the world you're a
true force to be reckoned with and have much to offer to
whatever situation you find yourself in. Whether you've
struggled with confidence or self-esteem in the past or still

wrestle with it today, here are a few simple suggestions to get more pep in your step and attain the self-assurance you need to enter any situation feeling good about who you are.

Pick your theme song. You may not be a movie star or have your own television show but that doesn't mean you can't have a theme song for your day-to-day life. A song that speaks to the very core of your being and perks you up as soon as you hear it playing. A song that makes you willing and ready to go out and take on the world and whatever it has to offer. It can be a slow song with soothing lyrics or one with a fast-paced beat that makes you feel like cutting the rug in the middle of your living room. Whatever music you favor, listening to your favorite song at the beginning of what will be—or the end of what has been—a trying day will lift your mood and remind you of who you really are. For truly inspirational songs try the quirky theme from one of Michelle's favorite shows, *Sex and the City*, or the world-saving-heroine theme from *Buffy the Vampire Slayer*. Another good pick is the aptly titled "I'm Every Woman"—either the Chaka Khan or Whitney Houston version will do.

Smile at yourself. Many times low self-esteem can be traced to the way you see your physical appearance. You won't start loving your looks overnight but if you take time to admire your face a little each day, you'll find features you're actually quite proud of. The next time you look in a mirror try taking a moment to pay yourself a compliment. Smiling improves virtually everyone's profile and it will do the same for yours if you let it. Remember how great you look when you smile and share that smile with everyone you see the moment you leave the house.

Own your accomplishments. If you're having trouble identifying your contributions to the world, make a list of the things you've done and are proud of. Don't stop at college or even high school; go back to winning the blue ribbon for the third-grade spelling bee if you must. Accomplishments have no expiration date. Penning an "I did that" list will remind you of what you're capable of and may aid you in pinpointing areas of strength you should focus more heavily on in the future.

Admit your mistakes, and keep it moving. The fastest way to halt your personal growth is by dwelling on past decisions and mistakes. Everyone messes up at one time or another. Replaying offenses in your mind serves no purpose except to bring you down. Don't hold on to it. Give yourself a break and never look back.

Honor your beliefs. It's wonderful to hear the thoughts and ideas of others, but make sure to have your own. Stick with them and share them with the world. Draw your own conclusions based on facts and valid information. Don't rely on others to shape your opinion of the world, other people or yourself for that matter. Listen to and learn from others, but always make up your own mind if you want to appear confident of your worth. Only you will have to live with the consequences of your decisions, so trust yourself and your actions.

Accept and distribute compliments with ease. Never dismiss the kind words of others. Be it a stranger on the street or someone you've known for ages, simply smile and say thank you. Whether they mean it or have a personal agenda, learn to value yourself enough to think others will notice you. Also keep in mind that if you want people to recognize you and your accomplishments, you need to be willing to do the same. As the saying goes, you can't get what you aren't willing to give.

Know you are a strong, independent woman, because if you don't, no one else will. In order to get noticed and have others pay attention to who you are, you have to get comfortable with yourself. Keeping that smile on your face even through adversity will display a drive and a maturity that's sure to get you noticed and earn you respect as well. The better you feel about yourself, the more you'll be able to stand out and leave exactly the impression you'd like.

Put on a Happy Face

Friends and family rarely questioned Michelle's ability to hold a crowd's attention and focus even as a child, which is probably why she was elected class treasurer in junior high and appeared in several high school productions. She didn't allow her extraordinary height or any limitations to prevent her from being fully present and accounted for in all aspects of her life. Friends say Michelle always stayed positive and avoided at all cost any thoughts of inadequacy.

Michelle was a realist of course but she also always saw the cup as half-full and not half-empty.

—Mellody Hobson, longtime friend of MO

Embracing the positive in matters regarding who she was wasn't always an easy task for Michelle, but she found a way to think only the best of herself each and every day. Take a cue from Michelle by making a point of waking up each morning with a spirit that is thankful for and appreciative of the life you have right now. Meditate on the day that is before you with positive thoughts of what joy the next twenty-four hours will provide you with and how you'll engage and impress anyone who crosses your path. Embracing a mind-set filled with gratitude and appreciation goes a long way in making every day a good day.

Keep the Negative Far Away

Even if you feel sure your self-esteem is through the roof like Michelle's seems to be, negative thoughts can still easily creep in and chip away at any leverage you may have thought you had over your own mind. Most of your negative thoughts can be put to rest with a little work, but you have to recognize them before you can do anything about confronting them. Here are the three biggest setbacks of the mind that can attack anyone at any time. Acknowledge them and then close and lock the door on them.

Thoughts of Inadequacy

Very few people are good at everything and it's fine to chastise yourself from time to time, particularly if you've done something that hasn't made you proud. But enduring thoughts of imperfection about the great skills, presence, and gifts you do own can do a lifetime of damage. Without going overboard, get a little cocky about yourself. Acknowledge what makes you special, and view the world and people in it as fortunate to have you around. You have a purpose for being here and it's your duty to find out what it is—without beating yourself up along the way.

Jealous Thoughts of Others

Sometimes it's hard to celebrate the accomplishments of others without feeling as though you've failed somehow. Resentment and jealousy can overtake your self-esteem and position you as an angry visitor in someone else's life and not the bright star of your own. Don't get caught up in someone's story or in how their journey has unfolded as compared with yours. That has no bearing on you and your future. Rejoice in the victories of others and use them as motivation to continue plotting and planning your own.

Forgiveness Issues

When you can't and don't forgive, the negative feelings that you retain dig a hole deep into your soul. That hole becomes the perfect dwelling place for anger and outrage to grow and can lead you to overthink and overreact to unimportant matters. Flying off the handle on a whim will only cause you to feel worse about yourself later and you'll struggle to understand why. The less time you spend holding grudges against anyone or anything, the more time you have to enjoy the beautiful life you're living. Free whoever has hurt you or mistreated you and feel your self-confidence soar.

Seek and You Shall Find

If you do require an extra boost of self-esteem, be assured you are not alone. Not everyone is privileged enough to be born with Michelle's tough-as-nails confidence or have it fostered in them courtesy of focused and committed parents like hers.

But any woman worth her salt—and that means you— won't allow her circumstances, no matter how dire, to deter her from the bright future very possibly lurking just around the corner. Far too many young women today decide that since the odds appear soundly stacked against them, there's little need to look beyond what their immediate surroundings have to offer.

Bad move. Limits for any reason and on any part of your life are definite no-nos whether they are imposed by others or by you!

Can you actually imagine a woman as savvy as Michelle not finding alternative ways to gain the confidence and self-awareness she needed to succeed, whatever her family structure may have been?

Get to Know the Powers That Be

Even with her strong support system, Michelle fully understood the benefits of seeking information and assistance from those in positions of authority and power. Teachers, school counselors, clergy, and other mentor-like figures are excellent examples of the extended family anyone, including you, can seek out and embrace on your road to self-discovery and self-realization. Who hasn't had a teacher say just the right thing at just the right time that immediately got you on track to complete an overdue term paper, finish a last-minute project, or pass a most dreaded test? Even the smallest hint of a compliment or a piece of solid advice from someone with real-life experience can give you the boost you need to truly feel good about your chances and focus on the future.

What's Age Got to Do with It?

Don't fret about your chances of succeeding if you're older than what's considered traditional school-attending years. It's never too late to create or re-create the person you'd like to be, and it's certainly never too late to find the inspiration to do so. Michelle's mother, Marian Robinson, didn't fulfill her lifelong desire to work as a full-time secretary until after Michelle entered high school. Though she'd always wanted to be a secretary, Marian Robinson's family encouraged her to seek a career as a teacher. That wasn't the career she dreamed of, so she married and raised a family before attempting to focus on doing what she really desired. Michelle learned a powerful lesson from her mother's example and you should, too. There's no expiration date on dreams and there's no mandate out there that demands you pursue your dreams in any particular order or at any particular pace within the course of your life. But there most certainly is a mandate that you not let your goals or dreams wither away.

Starting today, no matter your chronological age, put your thinking cap on and begin identifying your forgotten or dismissed plans, ideas and dreams for the future. If they've been on the shelf so long that you barely remember what they were, here's a fun exercise to jolt your memory.

Get Inspired

Though the Web wasn't around when Michelle was growing up, she did her fair share of research on women she admired. Michelle was a great admirer of the late Barbara Jordan, the first African-American woman to give the keynote address at the Democratic National Convention. As a teenager, she devoured as many books and articles about Jordan's background and achievements as she could, never suspecting her own brush with history and political fame would take her to many of the same places.

Pinpoint a woman (or women) you like and admire in the news, on television, or in your immediate surroundings, then get to work and start researching. Thanks to the modern-day wonders of technology, you can learn virtually anything you want (or don't want) to know about anyone with a speedy click of your mouse.

If the source of your inspiration is nearby, cruise the Internet and local newspapers for their appearances and lectures; if they're not, check YouTube and TED.com for video presentations or conferences featuring your person of interest. Either way, you'll get a chance to see and hear someone you're already familiar with or discover an entirely new inspiration.

With relative ease and in the comfort and privacy of your own home, you can quickly scroll through numerous Web sites and retrieve histories of women with the achievements and qualities you most covet. Be it a regular woman who accomplished something extraordinary in her life or an extraordinary woman who changed the world, you'll get amazing insight into what you'll need on your journey of self-discovery. This makes it an ideal way for any woman to find good role models and just right for the woman who wants and desperately needs guidance and information without judgment or commentary from others. Remember, this journey is yours and yours alone.

She-roes

Michelle's personal female heroes over the years have been powerful women who amassed amazing accomplishments and awards through intelligence, savvy, pure persistence, and hard work. Michelle took to heart many of the achievements of the late Barbara Jordan and Judith Jamison, a dancer and now-retired artistic director of Alvin Ailey American Dance Theater, and continues to use each woman as an inspiration in her life and work. Both women had uniquely impressive careers that spanned decades.

Michelle's own journey mirrored Jordan's life in ways the young Chicago girl could have never imagined as a child. Jordan began as a lawyer but her intense interest in politics led her to become the first African-American woman to serve in the Texas state senate in 1967. The nation got its first glimpse of the Houston, Texas, native when she encouraged the House Judiciary Committee to impeach then-president Richard Nixon. She would rise again to the forefront of the country when she became the first African-American woman to give the keynote address at the 1976 Democratic Convention. And like Michelle, Jordan desired to attend Harvard Law School, although lingering, negative attitudes toward race and gender prevented her from realizing that dream. Michelle would earn the opportunity some thirty years later to attend Harvard Law just like her hero wanted to. She would also deliver a memorable address at the 2008 Democratic Convention in Denver.

Jamison was another childhood hero of Michelle's. A photograph of her striking profile, complete with her signature cropped Afro, was prominently featured in the Robinsons' living room for most of Michelle's youth. Jamison's roots as a principal dancer in the world's most respected African-American dance company greatly inspired Michelle's desire for grace and poise, two traits Jamison possessed in spades. Michelle loved dance and performed with dance groups in both elementary and high school.

Choose role models who speak to you and your passions, no matter what they look like or where they hail from. Michelle drew inspiration from these extraordinary women and in her own way followed their lead. Do the same when choosing a woman to inspire and guide you. Her accomplishments may seem like something for you to aspire to right now, but as time moves on you may find out that you have more in common with your hero than you think.

Never Stop Learning from Others

Taking a cue directly from Michelle, do some devouring of your own. Dig deep to find the ways talk show queen Oprah Winfrey succeeded despite dropping out of college or how Hollywood producer Mara Brock Akil, creator of television shows like *The Game* and *Girlfriends*, landed her big break after beginning her career as a lowly production assistant. Study the fascinating career trajectory of magazine editor Tina Brown or that of Supreme Court judge Sonia Sotomayor. Don't worry that your ultimate goal isn't to sit on the highest court or to run and publish a national magazine; reading about and understanding the trials and tribulations of successful women in any field will give you facts, focus, and fuel to master the passion of your choice. Pay careful attention not just to their stories but to any insight they give on *how* they overcame life's many obstacles and think about how you can relate it to yours. Isolate the exact qualities, actions, and details you'd like to replicate and eliminate the ones you don't. By learning about women whose paths and accomplishments pique your interest, you may place a supersized idea in your subconscious that will spark the business, craft, or project that will change your life forever.

Go the Extra Mile:
Seek out a woman you admire and ask her how she got to where she is now. You'll find that the oral history is consistently more interesting than the standard bio.

She has a plan and a list for everything and everybody. She puts me to shame, and I'm the president.

—Barack Obama

Make a List and Check It Twice!

According to her friends, Michelle is the undisputed queen of creating lists for absolutely everything she does in life. Never a fan of the unknown, Michelle abhors being unprepared for anything, and that goes for long-range future plans as well as what's for dinner each night. The president has said his First Lady usually keeps a list of every task she must perform for the day, week, and month.

Though slightly obsessive/neurotic (yes, we all have our issues) Michelle's lists keep her day, life, and world just how she likes it: sane, organized, and structured. Those are three things she values dearly and you should, too. So get a notebook and start jotting down big and small things you'd like to accomplish as you set upon your journey to a newly improved you. Write down every idea, no matter how far reaching or far-fetched. You don't want to miss or forget a thing.

Drawing on the character traits and accomplishments of your role models, pull together your own personal blueprint to bettering the life you have now or upgrading to the one you've always known you deserve. Creating a list of goals may sound like a daunting task, but don't be intimidated. Pull out your hope chest of old and new aspirations. Your blueprint can include anything from the ideas you'd like to implement on a new project at work this week to your step-by-step design for redecorating your bedroom next month or even the wish list of guests for the late-night talk show that you're sure you'll have one day. View your blueprint as a friendly guide or a much-needed to-do list that you keep on you at all times. So slide it into your wallet, place it on your nightstand, or tape it to your bathroom mirror for easy and frequent viewing. Make sure the list goes wherever you go.

If you aren't challenged, you don't make progress.

—Marian Robinson

Rule of Thumb No. 2: Try Something New

Are you still unsure of what to do next or how to get started? Ask for and follow through on the advice of those mentors you've recently contacted and/or stayed connected with in your life. Have them recommend programs, events, or projects that align with your interests and personality. Then, without skipping a beat, promptly make plans to join in and take part. Hesitation and questioning will only delay or possibly defeat the goal of finding out who you are and what you're made of in the first place.

Michelle is known to love a good challenge, and with just a little innovative thinking and proper planning, it shouldn't take you long to find the right challenge for you. The challenge could be as incredibly simple and as fun as volunteering for the lead solo in your church's choir or auditioning for a small role in the community theater's production of *Cat on a Hot Tin Roof.*

Locating and/or actually creating opportunities won't just challenge you but will force you to rely completely on your own strength and character. Immersing yourself in new activities can reveal new talents you never knew you had while also doing untold wonders for your self-esteem, not to mention your social calendar. Can you say win-win?

Don't forget that in your dual quest toward finding yourself and becoming just a bit more Michelle-like, you're bound to encounter a few activities you aren't very fond of. You also may discover you aren't very good at them. It's all a part of the process. While attending Princeton, Michelle opted to forgo some of the more popular social clubs and begged out of one or two other groups after deciding their platforms and focuses didn't fit her interests. Only by trying something new can you discover what makes you tick and what doesn't. It's the one sure way to know what to keep on and what to check off your list of future goals and possible plans. By leaving your tried-and-true comfort zone, you can gain the self-assurance you will need to find, develop, and nurture the authentic you.

Go the Extra Mile:

If you just so happen to already possess a bit of Michelle's penchant for tackling all things head-on, volunteer to be a trustee at your church or run for your local school board or city council. These vital parts of government desperately need community involvement from people of all ages, walks of life, and experience. Your voice could be exactly the influence needed to get a beloved after-school program more funding or to get your neighborhood more streetlights, making your community safer. Imagine the sense of pride and accomplishment you'll feel after achieving a goal that makes life a little easier for others, not to mention the incredible boost of confidence that comes with a position where you can create major change.

Surprise Yourself

Do the exact opposite of what others expect of you. Not only will that create extra excitement for you, but you'll also become a fascinating mystery to everyone else. Years before, Michelle scoffed at the notion she should follow in the footsteps of her brother and play basketball because of her height. "I wasn't going to be typecast that way," she said. Instead, she satisfied her interest in sports by swimming, running, and boxing. She delighted in doing the exact opposite of what people thought she should or would do. Also on Michelle's list of unpredictable pleasures, checkers, the card game bid whist, and a good game of Scrabble.

Forgo the Easy Road

By the time Michelle was set to enter college, she was overwhelmed by multiple acceptance letters, courtesy of her honor roll grades and regularly demonstrated leadership skills. Several top schools located in the Illinois area offered the eighteen-year-old enrollment and full tuition. These were good schools, comfortably close to her home and the parents she was fiercely loyal to and cared for. But Michelle was at a pivotal point in her life and she knew that whatever decision she made then would impact her life forever. So, in true Michelle fashion, she took the plunge and followed in the footsteps of her older brother by attending Princeton University in New Jersey.

Attending an Ivy League university some eight hundred miles away from home would be a frightening undertaking for any young woman, no matter how steadfast her confidence or how fearless her demeanor. Embarking on a journey into the unknown would shake anyone's core, even someone as confident as Michelle. But running away from an amazing opportunity because of fear was never an option for Michelle, and when your amazing opportunity knocks, don't let fear stand in your way either.

Reality Check

Though her older brother was truly thriving at Princeton, Michelle was savvy enough to know that the experiences of a minority woman can and often do differ sharply from that of a minority man. Particularly when that minority man is a celebrated athlete playing college basketball, as Craig Robinson did. But that sobering truism wasn't enough to deter Michelle from taking a leap of faith into a brand-new existence filled with more wealth, power, and privilege than she'd ever seen in her young life. The ride ahead of her wouldn't be smooth or particularly pretty, but it would be a crucial building block in creating and preparing her for a future few could have predicted.

Woman Up

While at Princeton, Michelle was subjected to circumstances, issues, and challenges many surely believed ended years before she arrived. Racism reared its ugly head for the Chicago native from the moment she arrived on campus. During her freshman year, Michelle was assigned a roommate from the South whose parents in no way wanted their daughter to share a room with an "urban African-American."

"Princeton was a great place to be from," says Hillary Beard, a college friend of Michelle's, "but not always a great place to be if you were a minority student."

The mother of Michelle's roommate did all she could to have her daughter removed from the room she was sharing with the future First Lady and succeeded by the time their second semester rolled around. While Michelle has said publicly she was unaware of the exact circumstances surrounding the abrupt departure of her former roommate, friends say it was clearly racially motivated. Yet Michelle never let the ugliness of rejection for whatever reason affect her mood, spirit, or focus.

"If it upset her she never said," says Beard. "She took it with a grain of salt and kept it moving. She'd come too far to let something like that upset her and prevent her from getting the education she came there for."

Rule of Thumb No. 3: Shake It Off

While you may never experience an incident as ugly or as traumatic as someone disliking you because of your race, sexual orientation, or religion, you more than likely will encounter those who reject you for no good reason at all. Wherever you may be—at school, college, church, or even your nine-to-five—there's bound to be a person or circumstance that threatens to throw a monkey wrench into your perfectly plotted plans for a successful but drama-free future. Somehow, Michelle knew at the tender age of eighteen that she couldn't let someone else's issues, whether she knew their exact origins or not, derail her life plans or the positive feelings she had about herself. She had to shake it off. She had to go through it and get over it. "I just knew something was wrong when she left," Michelle recalled. "But I never knew what."

One thing she did know was that whatever problem her roommate and her roommate's parents had was theirs, not hers. End of story. You can only fix you. Years later, during Barack Obama's historic run for president of the United States, Michelle's former Princeton roommate and her mother were interviewed and admitted regretting their actions so many years before. They added they were rooting and voting for Michelle and her family to land in the White House.

Success is always the best revenge.

Never Stop Learning

While we don't all have Michelle's Ivy League pedigree, a quality education at any point is available to anyone. In your quest to find the best or better you, making the decision to enroll in additional classes at your local community college, junior college, or even online institution can go far in advancing you toward your overall goal. Taking courses that focus on subjects beneficial to your current job or that you're just fascinated with can do wonders for advancing your personal journey. After graduating from Princeton University, Michelle didn't hesitate to enroll in Harvard Law School as soon as she could. She knew a good education remained the surest way to achieve the life she wanted.

Even if you don't have a particular academic goal in mind, learning inside or outside the classroom forces your mind to process information in completely new ways. A night course or online class could expose you to the latest cutting-edge ideas and the most detailed information on any topic of note. No matter your field of choice or favored passion, never stop learning.

Michelle's parents taught her that being an attractive and well-rounded woman meant being a knowledgeable, well-read woman.
—Mellody Hobson

Reading Is Fundamental

If time, finances, or other unforeseen circumstances prevent you from committing to a course load, consider the most ef-

Go the Extra Mile:

Though it can be costly to enroll in classes online, with a little research you'd be amazed at the opportunities available to you for little to no money. Massachusetts Institute of Technology recently began offering MIT OpenCourseWare, all the materials most undergrads and graduate students have access to while enrolled at the prestigious university for a fraction of the price. With that generous offer you can actually afford to study anything you want at MIT. Consider taking a course in comparative media studies or in urban studies and planning. While at Princeton Michelle took French, history, African-American studies, and literature in an effort to expand her horizons. Empower yourself with knowledge. It's a great self-esteem booster and a wonderful way to advance to the next level of your career and life.

ficient way to gain the knowledge you seek: reading. With the invention of the Kindle, iPad, Nook, and countless other gadgets that download books in seconds, there's no excuse not to pick up a book. Amazon even has a genius button that allows you to download a sample chapter on your reading device of choice with hopes you won't be able to put it down.

Staff members, friends, and former teachers all recall Michelle's devotion to reading. The First Lady frequently discusses her favorite books along with those she loves to read to first daughters Malia and Sasha with children and guests who visit the White House. Michelle's reading list is as varied, complicated, and diverse as she is, including such favorites as Toni Morrison's *Song of Solomon,* Harper Lee's *To Kill a Mockingbird,* and Maya Angelou's *I Know Why the Caged Bird Sings.* Friends say Michelle recently found *The Immortal Life of Henrietta Lacks* by Rebecca Skloot a fascinating if disturbing read. Skloot details the ethical issues surrounding the case of a woman whose cancer cells have been used for decades of research, though her family has never been compensated. Michelle admits her list of favorite novels hasn't exactly expanded at the rate she'd hoped over recent years, and for good reason. "I simply don't have time anymore," she said during a recent interview. "The books I read these days are the ones Malia and Sasha bring home from school."

Many working women and mothers may face a similar issue; after all, there are only so many hours in the day. Still, unless you are traveling around the country several days of the week with your husband who just happens to be the president, try your best to carve out some quality time for a long date with a book of your choice. Explore each title or author on Michelle's list of classic novels then decide if they belong in your new and expanded library. For other suggestions, check out the *New York Times* bestseller list each Sunday. Michelle certainly does.

Read Like a Lady

Devouring the contents of all the books, newspapers, and magazines you can get your hands on is an excellent way to create a more well-rounded and smarter you. A real lady like Michelle is always aware of the most pressing issues occurring in the world around her. Sure, she may glance at and acknowledge a story on Halle Berry's newest hairstyle or the latest news on Jennifer Aniston's love life, but she'll also read and reread the stories detailing U.S. military operations in Libya or the current rate of debt increase stateside. There's much to learn from perusing your local newspaper or skimming a popular online news site. Even if you just remember the headlines, you're ahead of the game. Reading increases your vocabulary, your range of thinking, and your ability to speak intelligently regarding events happening thousands of miles away or right down the street.

Fraser Robinson always made sure he brought home a copy of the *Chicago Tribune* each day after work for his children to read. Michelle loved the news section while Craig preferred catching up on sports. Fraser's simple act of sharing the daily news with his children made a world of difference in their lives and continues to have an impact.

Michelle is said to study several newspapers before she begins her business for the day. Though the First Lady has a full-time staff to alert her of stories particularly pertinent to issues she's close to, Michelle has her own core publications she feels she must connect with daily. Her newspapers of choice give her a unique perspective on various subjects impacting the United States and the world at large. One favorite, *The New York Times*, is an excellent source for detailed explanations and analysis on politics and international news, not to mention it features a wicked style section Michelle loves and is often featured in.

USA Today gives short and decisive info on matters close

to home, while *The Washington Post* offers Michelle local perspectives on her current city of residence. Using Michelle's guidelines, seek out a local and national newspaper that cover all your basic informational needs.

Go the Extra Mile:

Sign up on your favorite national newspaper's Web site to have headlines e-mailed to you daily. It's a great way to discover new sections of the paper and keep up with what's going on around you.

Chapter Two
Using What You Have to Get What You Want

The things you want in life won't get handed to you. There is a lot of
opportunity out there. But you've got to want it.

—MO

*G*rowing up in a working-class neighborhood on the South
Side of Chicago, Michelle didn't quite have the luxury of
being entitled. She certainly didn't grow up aspiring to become or planning to be the First Lady of the United States.
Nor did she anticipate the arrival of some fabulously wealthy
man with just the right pedigree, ready to sweep her away
to the land of fame and fortune. Michelle was taught early
and often by her extremely pragmatic parents that anything
she achieved or received in life would be the direct result of
her own hard work and persistence. There could be no
other way.

Young Michelle took heed and used her parents' no-
nonsense advice to set the tone for her life and the future

she hoped to one day have. By the sixth grade Michelle had already skipped a grade and was chosen to participate in the gifted program at her school. This offered her access to French and biology courses that she flourished in. Expanding her love of culture and art, Michelle studied piano with her great-aunt three days a week. "She would play and practice until we made her stop," remembers Marian Robinson.

That same focused intensity continued throughout her junior and senior high school years, helping her get the grades she needed to go to college. Close friends remember Michelle as the "mature minded" girl who always possessed a clear purpose and a plan.

It was clear to me that drifting in mediocrity was never an option for Michelle.

—Reverend Jesse Jackson Sr., a family friend of the Robinsons

---

Sadly, some women seem perfectly content to pin their hopes, dreams, and fondest wishes all on meeting Mr. Right, a man so fair minded and giving, his only true focus and concern is to give the woman in his life all the desires of her heart through his hard work.

It's no mystery why countless modern women put so much stock into the notion that a wonderful life can only and easily be attained by meeting, marrying, or at the very least procreating with a man of means. Music videos, television, and tabloid magazines regularly tout all the perks and pleasures of living the good life simply by being a wife. Apparently membership in the wives' club can be effortlessly acquired simply by being a beautiful woman; wearing just the right form-fitting, barely there dress; and attending just the right VIP events. If your most thoroughly thought-out plan for a future full of happiness and accomplishment is riding on the hopes of a marriage proposal or on becoming a "baby mama"—preferably from or for someone handsome and loaded—it's time to snap out of it!

Here's why: Let's say you've got your eye on someone like Chicago Bulls star player Derrick Rose. The cold, hard facts are these: There are between three hundred and four hundred fifty men who play in the National Basketball League each season and only about two hundred of them actually play. Yep, that's it. Odds are you won't be hooking up with any one of them, let alone meeting them. Be clear that there are even fewer big-time movie stars, chart-topping rappers, or dimple-faced NFL champions on the market to plan your life around. So, on a purely practical, commonsense level, this is simply not a sound blueprint for your life.

Dreams can't be doled out to you by lovers or brought to you packaged neatly with a bow by fawning admirers. Dreams come true and goals are accomplished only when you've worked for and earned them on your own.

The only limit to the height of your achievements is the reach of your dreams and your willingness to work for them.

—MO

This isn't to say that you won't meet the love of your life and/or the future president of the United States on the way to creating and building the life you'd like to have. (Hey, Kate Middleton met Prince William at college.) But the only way to be certain you're in complete control of your own destiny is by putting in the work and not leaving it to chance or the NBA lottery. Betting on an impromptu meeting with George Clooney at the local minimart where he'll fall completely in love with you is not only leaving too much to chance, it's utterly insane. Any smart girl knows that George Clooney doesn't fall in love with anyone!

If you're really smart (and you are), you already have what it takes or can most certainly learn and take the necessary steps to get exactly where you want to be. It will require hard work and it may take a little longer to get it done on your own, but it will feel tons better knowing you arrived at your desired destination using your own brains and savvy.

You have to be impressed with all that Michelle accomplished before she even met Barack. Her résumé was excellent and so were her achievements. She's a smart girl. Any woman should want that for themselves.

—Diahann Carroll, Emmy-award-winning actress

Be an Independent Woman in Thought

It can be all too easy to compare yourself and the life you're currently living to those in your immediate circle and even those you see on TV every day. You know them well, or at least you think you do. The mega-success of social media has made it impossible to avoid becoming privy to the most personal details of friends, associates, and famous faces alike. You can then filter what's happening in their lives through your own personal experiences, and usually, it doesn't add up. Just as your mother may have told you, nothing is ever as good as it seems. Don't covet the so-called great lives of others; develop your own individual path that comes from being completely true to yourself. Throughout high school, college, and beyond, Michelle never yearned to travel the course someone else was already on. She moved forward with conviction and determination to the beat of her own drum and in the direction her spirit told her to go. In order to receive whatever pot of gold is meant just for you, you'll need to find a way to do the same. Take a few tips from Michelle.

Embrace silence. It can be quite difficult in today's world to have time to become comfortable in your own company. Cell phones, laptops, and media devices, along with connecting us to others, can become one more way to distract ourselves from our inner feelings and thoughts. Moments of calm or introspection are important mechanisms for our daily lives. Michelle was often seen chastising her husband for checking his BlackBerry nonstop while on the campaign trail. When the then-future president was relaxing with his kids and family, Michelle always insisted he turn everything off for just a while to be present. (She probably had to back off the suggestion of turning off his electronic devices when he became president, but the seed of not allowing electronics to overpower him was planted.) Break away from technology once in a while and learn to live in the now.

Stay humble and choose your spots well. Having strong morals and convictions doesn't mean you have to share them with the world at any given moment. Michelle is well-known for keeping abreast of the subjects affecting her husband's government as well as having strong beliefs and opinions on most things occurring here and around the world. The key to succeeding is knowing when and where to speak up. This is a lesson Michelle has had to learn through trial and error, particularly during her husband's first campaign. Michelle infamously told a Milwaukee audience in early 2008, "For the first time in my adult life, I'm really proud of my country. Not just because Barack has done well, but because I think people are hungry for change." Her strong words raised the eyebrows of more than a few people and she found herself accused of being anti-American. Michelle realized that it can be more useful to keep the core beliefs and ideals of your heart close to the vest at times. You can stand out as self-confident without forcing your beliefs on others. This behavior also emphasizes humility, an important facet of drawing people to you. When it comes time to speak your mind, choose your timing carefully.

Be a role model. If you carry an air of confidence and vitality, others will automatically be drawn to you. By simply being yourself and not sacrificing your morals, you can channel your inner talent into whatever you want to do. Independence takes strength and confidence, so suspend doubt and truly embrace yourself without question. Developing and focusing on goals you can accomplish on your own will do wonders, inspiring confidence in yourself. Once your optimism is channeled, you'll start to feel bolder by the minute and your life will begin to take on new meaning.

Michelle is the kind of woman I'm proud my daughter can look up to. She's a wife, mother, and professional woman and she makes it all look very easy, which anyone knows it isn't. Whenever she speaks, you know she has something worthwhile to say. You can't say that about everybody.

—Samuel L. Jackson

Embracing the Rewire

It's time to take real action about where you are headed. As a young girl, Michelle had vivid visions of becoming a pediatrician. Somewhere during her junior year in high school she began to fear her grades in math and science weren't as strong as they needed to be, so she changed course. Per usual, Michelle was earning A's and a few B's in those subjects, but anything less than perfection wouldn't do. Facing reality, no matter how harsh, was something Michelle took very seriously. Ever committed and focused on her pursuits, the future First Lady quickly turned to plan B, law. She pursued this new goal with relish. At Princeton, she majored in sociology and minored in African-American studies, while taking full advantage of more diverse subjects such as French, psychology, and Russian history. As she grew academically at Princeton, so did her view of the complex world around her. For her senior college thesis, Michelle described the harsh realities of having brown skin on the Ivy League campus. She made little attempt to sugarcoat her painful experiences in her aptly titled paper "Princeton-Educated Blacks and the Black Community." She bravely discussed the feeling of being a "visitor and of not belonging at Princeton" in the paper that would later receive major criticism from the Right during her husband's presidential campaign. As always, Michelle told her truth as she saw it and worried little about later consequences.

At Princeton, she also developed a deep passion for enhancing the life of others. At the Third World Center on campus she coordinated after-school child-care programs for the children of Princeton lunchroom and maintenance employees. She often enlisted her brother Craig's help to entertain and play with the young children. Friends in college remembered her loving bond with the children, which continued with many of them after she graduated. There would be no lapse in Michelle's drive after graduation. She had her heart set on Harvard Law School and that's where she headed in the fall of 1985. While she thrived in all her classes in law school, she truly stood out in the work she did outside the confines of school.

"Michelle really shined in the after-school program at Harvard," remembers her law school teacher Charles Ogletree. "She liked law school but she really worried about giving back to her community in Chicago. She wanted to do something worthwhile for those people she'd grown up with and those who needed it the most. Those thoughts were never far from her mind."

At the end of each day, Michelle would spend her time at the Harvard student-run legal aid office, which offered legal advice to poor clients who couldn't afford a lawyer. There, Michelle would advise clients on matters such as conflicts with their landlords, messy divorces, or child-support cases.

"Women really related to the way she carried herself and how she dressed and spoke in a professional manner but still seemed relatable," Ogletree remembers. "She was always prepared and engaged in them and their problems. She cared about them getting custody of their kids and getting child support. She cared that their homes were heated and not filled with rats."

Rule of Thumb No. 4:
Changing Course in Midstream

It takes a supremely confident woman to understand and to appreciate where she excels and where she doesn't. If you are truly focused on your future, brutal honesty with and about yourself must prevail. Michelle took stock early on and felt she didn't have the tools needed to become a physician, so no matter how much her heart was set on it, she was strong enough to trust her own instincts about her abilities and change course in midstream. Don't be stubborn. If it doesn't feel right, then it probably isn't right for you. It's better to change course now than to be a prisoner to the wrong dream or desire for the long haul.

> Her [Michelle's] strong presence is unmistakable. It blows you away. You feel it as soon as you meet her.
>
> —Magic Johnson

What Does a Confident Woman Look Like? You!

There's a saying that goes "Some girls are born winners." Don't believe it. Some women simply position themselves to win. So what separates the woman who wins and the one who doesn't? A large part of it has to do with killer confidence, something Michelle has in spades.

• If your cup doth not runneth over with confidence, fake it until you actually believe your own hype. Remember, confidence attracts not only people but opportunities as well.

• Make a list of all the things you're good at or all the characteristics you love about yourself. Display those characteristics whenever you can if you love them—others probably will, too. Use your intellect/humor/observational skills to your advantage whenever the chance arises, then step back and watch all types of doors open.

• Dress the part. People judge you by any number of other physical attributes that you may or may not have control over. Be sure to act on the ones you do. Michelle understood the importance of looking her best. So no matter how lethargic you may feel in the A.M., when you head out to face the world outside your door, make sure you're conveying the exact message you'd like the world to receive about you from head to toe.

Moving Forward from Where You Are

Though Michelle made a number of her most demanding and life-affirming decisions about where she wanted to be while still in high school and college, it's never too late for you to overhaul your thought process, particularly when it comes to your nine-to-five. Not in the job of your dreams? Are you feeling stuck in a dead-end position that's going nowhere fast and taking you with it? Then it's time to pull out your blueprint for life and regroup.

Remember, while there is no need to panic or beat yourself up over being a little sidetracked in your career, once you realize it, getting unstuck has to move up quickly on your to-do list. Now is the time to reference some of the very people and research you've already compiled so you can begin your odyssey toward that new job, or preferably that new and incredible career that matches your considerable talents.

The economy will always go through its ups and downs, and certain aspirations or financial realities may force you to redirect or postpone your leap into a new future until a more stable time. For Michelle, her desire to become a lawyer was in some part due to her wish to have what she deemed a true dream job. She imagined a perfect position that would provide a great income to pay her bills and to give her a more upwardly mobile life. Michelle would later discover that dream jobs aren't always that dreamy and that much more was needed in her search for meaningful employment than the appearance of success. Similar to many women, Michelle would have to endure a few jobs that weren't exactly perfect before understanding what fit best with her goals for the future. If you're not happy at your place of employment, a place you give so much of your time, the damaging effects won't be easy to mask or confine. Evaluating your options will help to ensure that the unhappiness doesn't flow over to your nonwork life.

Taking Stock

Understand that at some point everyone has a job they aren't very fond of or grow dissatisfied with over time. After graduating from Harvard Law School, Michelle landed at the top Chicago law firm Sidley Austin and immediately became a valuable go-to person at the powerful company. She specialized in marketing and intellectual property, which means she handled transactional and antitrust issues. She even counted the purple dinosaur Barney as a client, arranging and managing the trademark protection and distribution of Barney's toys and other merchandise. Her new position paid around $65,000 a year and afforded the then-twenty-six-year-old many of the objects and experiences that signified true "Buppie" success in the nineties.

"She would have been a superstar. We were all crazy about her," Newton Minnow, senior counsel at Sidley Austin, recalls. Michelle regularly admits she was seduced by having such an enviable, high-profile position and that it gave her a level of confidence. She added that the allure was reinforced by having extra money in her pocket and an opportunity to begin paying off her massive student loans (which would haunt her for years) "quick and in a hurry." Although she'd one day meet her Prince Charming at that very job, she had an earnest, though not overly surprising, change of heart along the way.

Only a few years into her successful law career, Michelle's beloved father died unexpectedly. True to her trademark privacy, few at her office even knew her father was ill, nor did she alert them when he died. He'd been battling multiple sclerosis for years but had been expected to survive a supposedly non-life-threatening kidney operation. Michelle was devastated by the loss. Just a few months later, one of Michelle's college roommates and good friends died of cancer at just twenty-five years old. The loss of two very important people at such a pivotal time in Michelle's life inspired an assessment and subsequent overhaul of her future and focus.

As Michelle explained in an interview shortly before her husband was elected president, "I was confronted for the first time in my life with the fact that nothing is guaranteed. Was I waking up every morning feeling excited about the work I was doing? I could die tomorrow, so I had to ask myself, is this how I want to spend my time? Would my father be proud of the choices I made?"

My sister feared very little for most of our lives. If she wanted to do something or try something new she would. No fear or reservations, she'd just do it.

—Craig Robinson

No Second-Guessing

Those life-defining moments caused Michelle to consider entering the realm of public service. Although she knew her desired new direction would involve a major pay cut and loss of social status, she firmly believed community service would ultimately afford her a greater sense of satisfaction. Consider the actions and thoughts Michelle struggled with before deciding what she wanted to do next. She didn't make a snap decision or quit immediately. She also didn't beat herself up over wanting to change lanes so soon after committing much of her time and resources to law school.

Michelle felt strongly that unfulfilled dreams and desires had a way of nagging the subconscious until they were eventually acknowledged and recognized. So why ignore them? She still took her time and gave what would be a major career overhaul the amount of attention and focus it deserved. As you grow and mature you may find you have more than one purpose or passion in life. Where is it written that you're destined to have one job or career forever? Michelle didn't believe that and neither should you.

The future First Lady had the mind-set and persistence

to alter her life path whenever she felt it was time to do so. She also trusted her own intuition on what type of work would bring her happiness and satisfaction. If you're lacking Michelle's fearless attitude toward taking chances and following change wherever it leads, try developing a foolproof method of role playing and decision making to aid you in pursuing old and newfound dreams with a vengeance.

Narrowing It Down

You'll be forced to make a vast variety of decisions during your lifetime. Some will have minor consequences, others will be huge and have the potential to throw your entire world into a tailspin. It helps to have a process to properly evaluate your options.

1. As obvious as it sounds, identify the decision that needs to be made as well as the objective or outcome you want to achieve.

2. Make a list of all the pros and cons of your options. Michelle had to decide whether she wanted to give up a lucrative, well-paying position in order to give back to those in need.

3. Weigh the probabilities of possible outcomes. In other words, what's the worst that could happen? What will happen if I do A, B, or C and can I live with the consequences?

4. Solicit opinions and obtain feedback from those you trust or who have had a similar situation to contend with.

5. When you have considered all of the above, make the decision!

There are no guarantees in life, and that includes any decisions you make concerning your future. Be prepared to accept the risks associated with making unexpected moves and be prepared to deal with consequences both good and bad. Truly channel your inner Michelle by relishing new opportunities and options.

Rule of Thumb No. 5: Always Give Your All

In her quest to keep her stellar reputation at the firm, Michelle made a point of never letting her work at Sidley Austin suffer as she pondered the future of her career in law. Even as she dove into the search for her new passion in life, she continued to handle her projects with the same top-quality performance she had since day one. This is essential when you are embarking on a new path. Don't phone it in at the old stomping ground, not even on your last day. Remain that brilliant person you've always been. You could be working on the game-changing project that leads to your next job. Remember these few commonsense rules to follow while you work on your exit plan.

> You have to practice success. Success doesn't just show up. If you aren't practicing success today, you won't wake up in twenty years and be successful, because you won't have developed the habits of success, which are small things like finishing what you start, putting a lot of effort into everything you do, being on time, treating people well.
>
> —MO

Manage Your Goals

While you should avoid using office time or office resources for side projects and personal issues, you should also take advantage of any free time when possible. Instead of eating at your desk checking your e-mail, go outside and use your laptop, smart phone, or plain old notebook to set tangible goals for your current job and a path to the next job. Next, create steps toward your goals that can be worked on every day. Decide you'll apply for no less than five jobs a week in your effort to find new employment. Create a timeline for organizing all your files before the week's end. Keep track of your progress and enjoy each step that brings you closer to your goals.

Network Your Way to Your Dreams

Michelle's change of direction and careers involved serious soul searching and lengthy talks with friends and family. It also required seeking out new names and faces for honest feedback. After informing a number of her friends of her desire to change jobs, a mutual friend gave her the name of Valerie Jarrett, the chief of staff for the mayor of Chicago.

We know the rest. Jarrett and Michelle would immediately form an unbreakable bond that continues to this day. Jarrett would also become good friends with Barack and introduce the couple to the upper crust of Chicago power. Ask someone you know and trust in the field you're interested in out to lunch and pick their brain about how they got to where they are and who you should know. Repeat as necessary. If you don't know anyone in the field you're interested in yet, use the tips from chapter 1 to find someone whom you'd like to get to know. Dream jobs are rarely advertised, so do make your job search and career goals known to anyone who may be able to pass the word on.

Mind Your Facebook

While today's latest technology in the form of social media has made everyday life a lot more fascinating, danger and pitfalls are often attached to this ever-growing presence. Michelle has mentioned on a number of occasions that she's no fan of media sites like Facebook or Twitter, though both proved quite beneficial to her husband's presidential campaign. She's even insisted that daughters Malia and Sasha won't be seen on social media sites for a long time if she has any say about it. Ironically Michelle did send her first official tweet in October of 2011 through the Joining Forces initiative, a group that aims to improve education, health, and employment opportunities for military personnel and their families. Keeping it strictly professional and proving the military is indeed a cause that remains close to her heart, the First Lady tweeted, "Military families serve our country too. Let's all show support by #JoiningForces with them, Get Involved: JoiningForces.gov—mo." A YouTube video captures the First Lady nervously typing that first tweet, no doubt worried that Malia and Sasha were watching!

As you continue on your path toward the career or goal of your choice keep in mind that more and more potential employers are using social network profiles to research the history and background of candidates applying for positions. In other words what you say and do on Facebook and Twitter can go a long way in hurting your chances or helping you facilitate your dreams for the future. According to Jobvite, a social recruiting company, 45 percent of all companies view the social network profiles of candidates, and those numbers are expected to soar to 89 percent of all companies in the coming years. If you already engage in social media activity, use the free publicity to your advantage and not your detriment.

Post updates related to your field of work and expertise to highlight how focused you are on your work and interests. Join groups and causes that speak to you and display your core values and beliefs. When posting pictures of friends and family, make sure they are respectful and reflective of the life you have and show things that you don't mind others viewing. While showcasing the best of you, avoid the use of profanity on your wall and instruct your friends to do the same. Go ahead and have high-spirited conversations with your friends near and far but don't have heated or intimate exchanges in public view. If something or someone has upset, hurt, or confused you, pick up the phone and handle it one-on-one. Public forums aren't the place to air personal disagreements or intense relationship chatter.

Lastly, try to make at least half or more of your posts about the world or the community around you. Show potential employers and your good friends that you're fully aware it's not all about you. If those ideas seem to take all the fun out of social networking, another smart option would be to create a Facebook brand page that allows you to keep your personal and professional profiles separate. Set up your personal profile so it's only available to friends and family. Then click on "Create a Page" to set up a brand or public-figure page for your professional identity. Try applications like BranchOut or BeKnown, which let you network with people on Facebook without having to make them "friends." For extra security, consider downloading Reputation.com's free uProtect.it tool, which encrypts everything you post to Facebook so your data won't get leaked the next time privacy settings change.

Be Creative

Some human resources representatives believe that traditional résumés will eventually be replaced entirely by user profiles on social networks. Much to Michelle's chagrin no doubt, establishing a sophisticated online presence will be necessary when Malia and Sasha begin their job searches. While Michelle may discourage the use of these sites, friends say she fully understands the importance of keeping up with what the tech world has to offer and how it can be used to further her work. She also gets her fill of hearing about the most up-to-date gadgets through her husband, Barack, who owns just about every item Apple has invented. Oldest daughter Malia shares her father's thirst for all things tech. Embrace the new tech age. Companies want to know that you can use social media so you can put your proficiency to use on the job. Get moving now with these ideas to develop and showcase your skills.

• Take control of what everyone sees when they Google your name by creating your own blog and/or Web site. Both will allow others to find you with ease and give you a chance to showcase your personal achievements. A blog will ensure a steady stream of content associated with your name and approved by you.

• Go beyond the traditional résumé by filming a two-minute video bio of yourself and placing it on your Web site and

YouTube. This gives potential employers a sense of your personality while also proving you're well ahead of the class in all things tech.

• Use social media to identify a connection with a job or career that fascinates you. Reach out to them for an honest online chat or e-mail, or better yet, ask if you can shadow them for a day to really get a feel for the job.

Mingling for, and with, a Purpose

Whether you're on the hunt for something new or are happy where you are, it can be easy to fall into the routine of expending your energy at your nine-to-five and wanting nothing more than to watch television and take care of the rest of your life when you get home. But you never know who you might meet, so the key is to never turn down an invitation. That means summoning all the extra energy you can muster after work or on the weekends for any and all dinner, cocktail party, or seminar invites that come your way. Don't be afraid to seek them out either! Who knows, the sister of the woman having a party in the apartment next to you may just work in human resources at the company of your dreams. Once you've committed yourself to attending the function of your choice, do make the most of it. Be approachable; spending the night talking only to the person you arrived with is not going to get you any closer to your goal. If you hear a lively conversation going on somewhere else in the room, make your way over and become engaged in the discussion, too. That will get you noticed quickly. If that's a bit too bold for you, find another loner in the room and introduce yourself. Remember the golden rule: Networking can occur just about anywhere—from revival night at your church to a coast-to-coast flight.

Once you start conversing with others, it's imperative to have something to say. And no matter how interesting you are, it cannot be all about you. Keep up with and stay on top of industry and world news. If someone brings up a topic you're not familiar with, don't wing it with answers you're not sure of. Instead, ask, "What do you think about that?" to deflect any awkward attention away from yourself while giving someone else a chance to pontificate on issues they are invested in. Make sure to listen to what is being said and avoid moving on to another subject before everyone who seems interested in contributing has. Also, don't forget to utilize one of Michelle's most endearing qualities (according to friends and associates)—be genuine. Being professional doesn't mean putting on an act. Don't feel the need to agree with opinions or ideas that go against your core beliefs. People usually see through that anyway. Networking isn't just about collecting a few cards and tucking them in your purse, it's about sparking and building key professional alliances and relationships.

The Art of the Conversation

Beginning conversations with new faces can be a daunting task. Most people understandably find walking into a room of unfamiliar faces and joining the conversation cold about as appealing as a trip to the dentist. Michelle and her husband are said to be masters at making people feel welcome and comfortable on any occasion, an art they've both perfected since being in the White House.

Actress Kerry Washington has visited the Obamas at the

White House several times and admits she's constantly amazed by the warmth and grace they both show all who enter their presence and home.

"I can remember being at the White House in 2009 with Alicia Keys for an event for women and young girls in the DC area and I was so in awe of how Michelle took time with every girl there," Washington recalls. "There were about fifty or sixty of them and she took the time to hug and encourage them all. She didn't stop until she'd embraced each one of them. The way the faces of those girls lit up while talking to Michelle was just so heartwarming. She was there for them. To see and feel Michelle's compassion and genuine desire to find a real connection with other people was amazing to watch and inspiring to feel."

Use Michelle's technique as inspiration when meeting someone new by showing sincere interest in the new face before you. Try to stick to small, lighthearted, and fun topics as you begin your chat. Politics, religion, and other issues should be introduced only after taking the pulse of the people in the room—if at all. Check below for a few simple, no-stress ideas for jump-starting truly enjoyable dialogue with others.

Find someone with an agreeable face. Be on the lookout for someone who looks open to conversation. If you're attending a social event given by a friend but you don't know anyone else on the guest list, ask the person nearest you when and where they met your mutual friend.

It's all in the details. When meeting new people, make a mental note of names and then use each person's name every time you reference them or ask a question. This shows you're thoughtful and focused.

Pose a question. Asking someone about something as innocent as family or the weather may sound cliché, but these are topics everyone has an opinion about.

Take it to the next level. If climate talk is a hit, move on to current events but take it slow. Ask what the hot topics were on the news today and then allow someone else to fill in the blanks.

Make a statement. Comment to others on your thoughts on a particular painting or sculpture in the home or establishment you're in. If all else fails, compliment the person's dress, suit, or hairstyle. A genuine compliment easily flows into questions about someone's favorite stores and the very best places to find the great deals in town. Keep in mind that next to being asked about family, the comment people love to hear most is something positive about themselves. Michelle is the master of quickly gaining people's trust and confidence by utilizing simple, commonsense rules of connecting. Do the same and your Rolodex will increase twofold in no time.

Go the Extra Mile:
Make an effort to attend at least one event every other month, whether it be a networking cocktail hour, a lecture by someone in the field you're interested in, or an event hosted by a charity that you support, where you may meet people you never would have otherwise who share your interests.

The Anatomy of the Perfect Thank-You Note

Michelle believes that being gracious is a must no matter the circumstance, and saying thank you is a major part of that progress. Just as her mother taught her years before, Michelle wastes no time in writing personal notes to the many people who've crossed her path at work, during her husband's campaign, and since entering the White House. During the 2011 unveiling of the Martin Luther King Memorial in Washington, D.C., many guests had to wait for long periods of time to be transported by bus to the White House celebration. Michelle made a point of thanking all who'd waited that day for their patience and sent notes thanking them once again for their kindness and understanding in the days that followed. Michelle's motto is that a note of thanks needs only to be genuine and heartfelt, not long and overly sentimental. Develop this practice of Michelle's and send thank-you notes that are eye-catching, sincere, and memorable.

1. Always use classic stationery for business purposes. Neat penmanship is an integral part of the written expression. It can make or break you as a prospective employee. The person on the receiving end will appreciate the thought of a solid, handwritten, and professional-looking note.

2. Draft a formal note with a greeting, body paragraph stating your thankfulness for having met

the person and eagerness to continue your conversation, conclusion, and signature. It should be simple and concise.

3. Add personality. This is a vital element that belongs mostly in the last paragraph before the closing statements. It's respectful to thank the reader for any suggestions, considerations, or advice you were given, but remember to speak to the unique experience you had with the person. If it's for an actual job interview, mention the exact position and how you look forward to hearing from them in the near future.

4. Proofread twice. To refrain from mistakes such as misspellings, incorrect grammar, or redundancy, reread your note again and again. Use a thesaurus and dictionary if you have to, and ask a friend to proof your note one last time before sending.

5. Time is of the essence. Make sure to send your note off in a timely manner—no more than a day or two after the initial meeting or interview. This shows that you're punctual, persistent, and courteous.

If you're firmly a part of the new generation that insists on using e-mail for all communication, send away if you must. But follow up with a handwritten note as well. The combination of the two will convey the positive impression you desire.

Rule of Thumb No. 6: Sharpen Your Skills

While you bide your time and make the most of those must-have connections you'll need for future job satisfaction, make sure to exercise your most valuable possession—your brain! Take advantage of the resources out there that are meant to help people refocus and cultivate their new careers, and learn something new. The best part? The majority of these resources are free.

Develop your computer skills. No matter how long you've worked for a company, it's important to keep up-to-date on new software skills. If you need a quick computer tutorial, refer to GCFLearnFree.org to improve your basic technology skills. If there's a new program you'd like to learn, try downloading its free trial to become more comfortable using it, or sign up for a course for a full tutorial. Learning updated software will enhance your professional skills and add diversity to your experience and your résumé.

Enhance your writing and communication skills. Check out Web sites such as MindTools.com or Khake.com. These sites offer advice on how to protect your employability and transform your professional life through improving your communications skills such as grammar and vocabulary.

Nurture your public-speaking skills. Check with local colleges for courses on public speaking or Toastmasters International meetings. Group members can give you meaningful feedback that will help in your next office meeting.

Michelle thoroughly immersed herself in the low-income community around Harvard and their needs while she was in law school. She helped anyone she could and took a sincere interest in those people's lives and circumstances. I fully expected her to become a senator or serve in political office because she was so concerned with improving the lives of others.

—Charles Ogletree

Giving to Get

Volunteering can be a particularly valuable tool in assisting you in finding your passion, while also impressing potential employers. People take notice of selfless acts. Michelle's volunteer work no doubt influenced her desire to later pursue public service. At Princeton University Michelle spent a great deal of her time outside of class at the college's community center, where she spearheaded an after-school reading program for children of the university's manual workers. At Harvard she guided low-income residents unable to afford legal advice and representation on issues ranging from divorce, child support, and custody issues to tenant laws. Though she would take a job with a high-paying law firm after graduation, her days of volunteering were never far from her mind and continued to influence her decisions and professional goals years later. Continuing her desire to give, the First Lady made an appearance in 2011 on *Extreme Makeover: Home Edition*, where she helped expand a community center for homeless veterans.

Already inspired but not sure where to start? VolunteerMatch .org allows you to upload your résumé to be connected with a host of companies in your area in need of your exact expertise or skill. The program also provides you with an e-mail account that sends you updates on possible future matches and makes it easy to encourage friends and family to join you. While working in an area familiar to you makes perfect sense, don't be afraid to step outside of your comfort zone and try something that challenges you in new ways. If you're usually behind a desk, try volunteering with children outside at a local community center. You may find that teaching is where your true passion lies.

Whichever area you choose, realize the only way of getting the most from your volunteer experience is by giving it your all just like Michelle. Approach the act of volunteering as you would a job by making a commitment to be there at the agreed-upon times and arriving ready and willing to do what's needed. Appreciate the free experience you're receiving from a brand-new world while also acknowledging the positive impact you're having on someone else's life. Ultimately your experience will expand not only your résumé but your view of the real world around you. Not to mention you're bound to meet and develop connections with interesting people.

Chapter Three
What About Your Friends?

We should always have three friends in our lives—one who walks ahead who we look up to and we follow; one who walks beside us, who is with us every step of our journeys; and then, one who we reach back for and we bring along after we've cleared the way.

—MO

Friends, the actual company you keep, can reveal a great deal about you, where you are in life, your mind-set, and the world you live in.

One of Michelle's most intense beliefs over the years revolves around the notion that the greatest asset a woman has is her ability to bond and build friendships with other women. In Michelle's world her girlfriend network is her lifeline in both good and bad times. Ever the reason to choose your most trusted social companions as meticulously as you would your future husband.

Good friends, like good husbands, can lift you up above

the clouds, and bad ones can do exactly the opposite. Friends can be your much-needed life vest in the midst of a raging storm or that unwanted push when you're right on the edge. Friendship, the kind you give as well as the kind you receive, depends largely on what you're willing to do to obtain, maintain, and retain it. Every relationship in your life requires work—hard work—and girlfriends are certainly worth it. Studies have proven that women need relationships with other women because those bonds boost emotional, psychological, and physical health.

Strong, lasting friendships can supply you with amazing experiences, unbelievable adventures, and nonstop laughter in your life. But they can't and won't last very long if they don't include women who share your core values and attitudes.

Ties That Bind

Sista friends became a crucial mainstay in Michelle's life very early on. Even as a teenager growing up in Chicago, Michelle doted on her close high school friend Santita Jackson, the daughter of civil rights leader Reverend Jesse Jackson Sr. Michelle fondly recalls spending many afternoons in the Jackson home hanging out with Santita and the rest of the Jackson clan after school. The two women were so fiercely close and loyal to one another that Santita served as Michelle's maid of honor at the Obamas' wedding and even sang an old Roberta Flack song at the reception. Santita is also godmother to Michelle and Barack's oldest daughter, Malia. One of the most obvious ways Santita has continued to demonstrate the strength of her friendship with Michelle is by having little contact with the press to discuss their longtime connection. She's protected her bond with her high school classmate with a vengeance and continues to visit and associate with the Obama family on a very private basis, away from the prying eyes of the public.

It was fun watching Michelle and my daughter grow up and enjoy the school years. They had the same interests and enjoyed the same things, which is how friendships are born and thrive.

—Reverend Jesse Jackson Sr.

Through the years, Michelle has amassed long-lasting female friendships from virtually every circle she's entered. In college, law school, and her various places of employment it proved invaluable for Michelle to connect with other women who shared similar ideas and dreams and equally progressive ways of achieving them.

Michelle's friends very well may have similar personality traits, but they also happen to come in all ages, colors, and sizes. In the Robinson household, she was taught that people are people, no matter their physical makeup. Because Michelle's gal pals come from such an assorted mixture of nationalities and backgrounds, she's gotten a bird's-eye view of cultures and traditions fascinatingly different from her own. Friends can show you the world without the need of ever standing in those dreaded lines for a passport.

Have you ever been to a seder? Observed Ramadan? Celebrated Cinco de Mayo? If you haven't the slightest idea what any of these cultural references mean it's time to expand your friend territory! True sisterhood transcends everything, including skin color.

My ability to get through the day greatly depends on the relationships I have with other women. We all need that community in our
lives, but it is difficult to create if we are unable to sustain meaningful relationships with women. We have to be able to champion
other women. We have to root for each other's successes and not
delight in one another's failures.

—MO

Rule of Thumb No. 7: Like Minds

Search for and embrace female friends who understand you
and the goals you've set for yourself in life. Without that you
run the very real risk of having people in your immediate
surroundings who are unable to give you the support you
need to achieve. Worse than that, having people around you
who resent you and any plans you may have is a recipe for
failure. Michelle's inner circle rotates heavily around a vast
variety of women from all types of backgrounds and walks of
life. Though their life journeys may differ in some ways, they
are all linked by their shared quest for higher education,
strong family ties, and cultural pursuits. That's not to say
your friends have to be virtual mini-yous (that would be
rather boring, though slightly amusing for a short time), but
the friendship will be a lot stronger and last a lot longer if
you're not complete worlds apart.

A Friend Indeed

Of all the amazing benefits that come along with true friendship, and there are many, none is more fulfilling than having a gal pal who makes you feel good about yourself—a friend who knows exactly what to say or not say regarding your weight, hair, or outfit on the eve of a big job interview or that date with Mr. Right. Or the friend who reminds you of just how smart and talented you really are even when you receive that rejection letter from a school, hiring manager, or ex-boyfriend. Michelle's self-confidence and self-esteem have roots in many places, but the positive friendships she shares with her close female confidants no doubt contribute immensely to her overall sense of self. No one friendship will give you everything, but with any luck, you'll find and keep a variety of women in your life able to offer you exactly what you need when you need it most.

The Five Girlfriends All Women Have to Have

The "For Real" Friend

This is the friend who knows more about you than anyone else. Maybe it's because you've known her as long as Michelle has known Santita, or maybe it's someone you met later in life but have shared everything with. This is the friend who is most concerned about you and who will do whatever it takes to help you. She's the friend who'll tell you that you look a hot mess before you even think of stepping foot out of your house or will call you out when your behavior is totally unacceptable in public. She may drive you a bit batty at times, but you know her comments and guidance are always coming from a place of love and support. Put simply, this friend wants to see you at your best at all times. Why not call her up right now and let her know how much you appreciate her?

The "Down for Whatever" Friend

She's the friend you call when you want to try something new. Whether you're planking, roller skating, or learning a foreign language, this friend is always ready to go. Yvonne Davila, a twenty-year friend of Michelle's, is the perfect example of this. She kept Michelle company during Barack's senate runs and spent time with her when Barack left the country to work on his first book. Every woman loves a friend who's willing to join in on a spur-of-the-moment adventure. Not only is she a lot of fun, but her friendship encourages your growth and helps you tackle your fears. Get in touch with her to see if she's interested in helping you conquer one of the goals on your new list from chapter 1, or maybe she'll have the perfect new challenge in mind. Salsa dancing?

The Loving Friend

This friend may not be your mother, but she could step in if need be. She's never too busy to listen to your relationship issues, family drama, or career plans. She always has a kind and supportive word or comforting hug for you no matter what's going on in the world. Her actions speak louder than words ever could and those actions scream love. She's a true nurturer and she can be a crucial lifeline for you when times get rough. Make sure to return the favor; call her up and see how she's doing. Michelle's longtime friend and former boss Valerie Jarrett occupies this role in her life.

The Keeper Friend

This friend is the keeper of all your secrets. All women need someone in their lives whom they can comfortably tell their deepest and darkest secrets without fear of their being repeated to the outside world. Whether it be the surprise birthday you're planning or that personal issue you're dealing with but don't want everyone to know about, she listens and keeps it to herself. No easy task. Verna Williams, an old school friend from Harvard Law School, fits this description to a T for Michelle. She was the first friend Michelle told she'd met the man she'd one day marry. Why not plan a day together where *you* keep the secrets—of where you're going to eat and what hot night spot you're going to afterward!

The Warrior

The friend who protects you and your interests at all costs. The one who makes sure you are taking care of yourself and who will confront anyone who confronts you. You're always right in whatever situation you find yourself in according to this friend and she'll go down fighting for your good name to the end. These friends aren't easy to find. For Michelle, her mother, Marian Robinson, is that friend.

No one person can be everything you need as a friend, lover, or anything else. Understanding and recognizing what you have to offer as a friend and what your friends realistically have to give back will go a long way in making the most of your girlfriend network, not to mention reducing hurt feelings and/or disappointments.

Mind Your Words

When confiding in even your closest girlfriends, it's important to recognize what tidbits of life are appropriate to reveal
and which ones to hold on to. Oh, yes, it does feel wonderful
to talk for hours to your favorite buddy about all the matters
of your heart, head, and life. That's what friends are for, right?

Absolutely!

But being a bit stingy with some of your life's most intimate details isn't so much a show of mistrust for a girlfriend
as it is a show of respect for yourself. So think twice before
giving your girlfriends an overly thorough rundown of your
love life. Telling them you're very satisfied and very happy
with your relationship should do. You can never be sure that
even the most well-intentioned friend won't have an innocent
slip of the tongue at the wrong time or place, like in front of
your partner or parents. That would cause untold embarrass-
ment for all. Suffice it to say, certain joys of life are best kept
to oneself.

Similarly, monitor the complaints you share about your
current love interest. Your mate's small offenses will seem
minor to you in a few weeks but may not be so easily forgotten by dear friends. Unless it's something major that you
need a friend's opinion on, or something you don't mind a
total rehashing of weeks down the road, deal with your mate's
little annoyances on your own.

Our friendship was formed from the moment we met that day.

—Valerie Jarrett

A Friend for the Long Haul

Michelle and Valerie Jarrett's paths crossed during a major transition in Michelle's life. After leaving the world of corporate law in 1991 to pursue work opportunities in the public sector, Michelle decided to interview for a position in the mayor of Chicago's office. Jarrett, a well-connected lawyer and businesswoman, was the deputy chief of staff for then-mayor Richard Daley and handled most of the hiring for his staff.

Surprise, surprise, Jarrett was so enamored with Michelle's sly wit and quick smarts that she offered her a position on the spot. Ever cautious in her decisions, Michelle had one request of Jarrett before agreeing to accept the job—she wanted Jarrett to meet her fiancé, Barack Obama. The three soon broke bread and within months, Jarrett, a high-society darling of sorts, had introduced the young couple to many of the most prominent and wealthy citizens in Chicago. Those well-placed introductions would later prove essential to Obama's short- and long-term political pursuits.

In fact, the Obama/Jarrett friendship produced much fruit for both parties. Jarrett would later serve as the cochair of the Obama-Biden presidential transitional team and senior adviser to Obama's presidential campaign. She now serves as a senior adviser to President Obama. Though it should never be the main objective of your connection with people in your life, never underestimate where having and being a good friend can take you.

On the Flip Side

Just as good friendships can open doors for major new opportunities and unexpected windfalls, wonderful chances can also turn into painful disappointments. Case in point: Longtime Obama family friend Desiree Rogers was appointed White House social secretary by President Obama in 2008. Unfortunate circumstances required Rogers to leave that position prematurely, which could have put an uncomfortable strain on her friendship with Michelle. Smartly, both women were wise and mature enough to understand that when it comes to business, it should never ever become personal. The reality of life is that even if a dear friend does manage to hook you up with the job of your dreams, it's still not guaranteed to pan out exactly the way you'd like. Not surprisingly, Desiree was less than pleased at losing such a wonderful and history-making position, but she didn't blame her good friend for the unfortunate end. She took the high road and Michelle was grateful for it.

Neither woman let a rather difficult situation get the best of their friendship, and you shouldn't either if faced with a similar predicament. Michelle and Desiree continue to enjoy a healthy bond to this day and still share mutual friends and connections. Consider the alternative if these two women hadn't been able to put their issues aside for the sake of friendship. Their saga would have no doubt gone on to make fabulous fodder for the countless tabloids and less savory news shows. Choose friends who understand that true conflict resolution is best handled one-on-one and not in front of an audience.

Walking in the dark with a friend is better than walking alone in the light.

—Helen Keller

Don't Believe the Hype

Tune in on any given day to a reality show of your choice and you're destined to see women of all backgrounds, races, and intelligence feverishly disagreeing over a man or actually physically roughing one another up due to any number of issues. Audiences seem to enjoy a good old-fashioned catfight and the new female faces of reality television seem quite happy to oblige. What television networks enjoy are huge ratings and they're not all that concerned with how they get them. If there's big money to be made by showcasing women willing to degrade themselves with fist fights, hair pulling, and verbal insults on national television, so be it, right?

Wrong.

The misguided illusion that women, and particularly women of color, can't get along with one another due to any number of petty jealousies and insecurities is not only untrue, but it's a particularly dangerous message for all young women still attempting to master the fine art of navigating their own friendships. It can also send just as troubling a message to any woman of any age who is still struggling with exactly how to develop solid female bonds.

"What young girls and all women to some extent are learning today is that another woman is a not a friend, but always an enemy," says Dr. Gail Wyatt, professor of behavioral studies at UCLA. "That sets up a lifetime of distrust and mistrust of people of the same gender. It eliminates the chance for a womanly bond."

Don't kid yourself. There will always be some valid reason to mistrust a few of the women you'll meet along life's way. Yes, it hurts to be lied to and talked about by a girlfriend you thought sincere. But don't let a bad experience rob you from fully appreciating the joy of having other women in your life. Michelle's never been seen giving the side eye to the other wives of foreign heads of state and she enjoys the friendships she has with many women. You wouldn't kick all men to the curb because of the heartbreak or rejection inflicted by one man. The same rule should apply for girlfriends as well. Mimic Michelle's no-nonsense approach to everything she encounters by taking the necessary precautions when deciding who should and shouldn't enter your inner circle. By using your smarts and basic common sense, you can sidestep the majority of arguments thought to plague female friends.

Rule of Thumb No. 8: Just Say No

Michelle never fails to emphasize the importance of strong female relationships to anyone who'll listen, particularly her two young daughters, Malia and Sasha. To that end, a source within the White House reveals that Michelle insists her daughters not watch any shows that depict women belittling each other or themselves. Translation: little to no reality television. Michelle tries to enforce the no reality tv rule regularly but admits to friends that it can be very difficult to monitor her girls' viewing habits when friends come over or if they have sleepovers at a classmate's house. "She does what she can to make sure they don't waste time watching complete mess," says the source. "Barack really hates for them to watch that trash and the little they do see doesn't include women using violence against each other. Michelle won't have that."

Maybe you shouldn't either. As much as you may try to deny it, your brain regularly retains a great deal of mess from the outside world—mess you don't need and mess that isn't at all beneficial to your overall being or your plans for future success. While many consider the regular consumption of shows such as *Basketball Wives* or *Mob Wives* a guilty pleasure, never underestimate how easily the underlying negative message of such shows can float into your mind, take root, and flourish. And in the same way you might avoid these shows, there may be certain types of "friends" to steer away from too, in order to ensure that you are growing strong friendships.

Five Girlfriends a Woman Should Avoid— Michelle Certainly Would

The Woman with No Girlfriends

Any woman who doesn't have other girlfriends and brags about it is probably guilty of the same behavior she finds so appalling in other women. If she doesn't befriend other women as a rule, don't attempt to become the exception. It's not worth it. Move on.

The Drama Queen

There are some women who live for drama in their lives and don't mind passing their mess on to whoever happens to be around. Don't let that be you. Stay away from this type of woman. She's the woman who always seems to be having trouble with someone in her life and one day it will be you. Who needs it? You don't.

The Narcissist

This woman thinks the world is her stage and she's the only star. She thrives on being the center of attention and fumes when anyone else steals her thunder. She sucks the air out of a room, which means there's none left for you or anyone else. When you see her coming, run—don't walk—the other way.

The Hang-up Girl

This woman is so filled with so many insecurities she can barely contain her dislike for others because of their looks, possessions, or any number of reasons. She projects her own unhappiness onto others, and that includes you. No thank you. Keep it moving.

Ms. Needy

This woman doesn't understand the basic give-and-take foundation of friendship. She always needs a shoulder to lean on, money to borrow, or some other favor, like purchasing a last-minute ticket for her to Maui. Of course, she can never be found when you need the same from her. Next!

Quid pro Quo

Now that you have identified the individual roles and significance of friends in your life, you can turn your full attention to how to nurture and maintain the bonds you share. Follow your heart and instincts. A great deal of what it takes to sustain friendships comes down to simple common sense and logic. Treat others in the same manner you'd like to be treated, and be extra thoughtful and kind to your besties, like Michelle. She is known for putting her party-planning skills to use by throwing baby showers, dinner parties, and congratulatory soirees for those near and dear at the drop of a hat.

Thank You for Being a Friend

Being a great girlfriend isn't just about being there during big life moments. It's also about being thoughtful in the everyday. Keep the following in mind when it comes to your friends.

Just listen. When a girlfriend comes to you with a problem, your first instinct may be to instantly try to figure a way out or a solution for them. Noble, but not always necessary. Sometimes a friend just wants another friend to listen, not make all their problems go away. A nod, a smile, or simply agreeing that she needs a new job or a new man may be all she wants and needs. So when a friend tells you they need a shoulder to lean on, give it to them. Listen as they let it all out and then allow them to ask you for advice. If they do, have at it and give them the benefit of your wisdom.

Tell her she looks great. Everyone can use a kind word or a sincere compliment from time to time. Make sure your girlfriend knows when she's killing them softly with her new haircut or that one-shoulder Diane von Furstenberg dress you'd like to borrow sometime. A few positive words from you can make her day.

Take the helm for the night. Every woman deserves a carefree good time now and then. Gift your girlfriend with a night on the town filled with all the fun, food, and drinks she can handle. Let her have the time of her life while you take the responsibility of navigating the night and getting everyone home safely. Allowing her time to get away and forget the troubles of the day or the week is worth more than a thousand gift certificates to Bloomingdale's.

Take the kids. If your girlfriend has children and rarely has time to think straight, much less get a manicure or haircut, offer to take the kids for the morning or the day. Parenting is tough whether single or married, so any offer of assistance is usually greatly welcomed. Giving her a few hours of free time to sleep in, shop, or just watch the Home Shopping Network in peace is truly a gift that keeps on giving.

Never say "I told you so." Another way to be the best girlfriend you can be is by simply going along for the ride of life without judgment. So when the guy you just knew was all wrong for her finally shows his true colors or the job she thought was a dream turns into the nightmare you always saw coming, zip your lip. Real friendship doesn't involve keeping score or reveling in another's mistakes.

Got to Be There

Michelle is the master of knowing just what to say to a friend when times are rough. The current First Lady is so devoted to her friendships that she's even willing to endure a bit of heat for one in need.

In 2010, the First Lady was bombarded with stinging criticism for taking a trip to southern Spain with her daughter Sasha and a few close friends, including Anita Blanchard, an ob-gyn who delivered both Malia and Sasha. Michelle thought the trip to the Mediterranean coast would aid in consoling her dear friend Anita, who'd recently lost her beloved father. Michelle didn't attend the funeral (which was in many ways quite thoughtful on her part—given the uproar her Secret Service detail would have caused at such an event), so instead she opted to spend some time with Anita on a trip abroad.

Unfortunately many didn't understand or fully appreciate the First Lady's thoughtful gesture, so harsh judgment quickly filled editorial columns and newscasts for days on end. Politics no doubt fueled many of the opinions on Michelle's trip to Spain, with most pundits citing the country's poor economic state as reasons for their disapproval. Though Michelle and her friends paid for all their travel costs and hotel accommodations, taxpayers were responsible for the Secret Service detail mandatory for the First Lady during all travel and at all times. Michelle also met with the president of Spain while there.

"Michelle just thought it was important as a dear friend to do this," said one of the First Lady's traveling companions. "It hurt to hear the criticism, but she was really thinking of someone else."

In true Michelle style, she weathered the storm of temporary public disapproval while spending important personal time with dear friends and family.

Rule of Thumb No. 9: Stick with It

According to those close to the First Lady, she never second-guessed her decision to travel to Spain with friends, despite loud cries of discontent from certain segments of the country. She accepted the consequences that accompanied it. Some of the decisions you make in life won't go over well with everyone, but if in your heart you feel you're doing the right thing, stick with it, deal with it, and never look back. Especially if it means choosing to be there for a friend in need.

While meeting up with friends at a resort in lovely Spain may not fit your reality right now, don't fret. There are countless other ways to snag memorable moments with girlfriends in times of celebration or sorrow. Carving out quality time for your gal pals, whether over lunch or on a cross-country trip, can offer seriously therapeutic benefits for you and all others who tag along.

She was just kicking it with her girlfriends, laughing, and having a good ole time . . . a regular girl out with her girls. They came backstage and you could tell the love she had for her friends and for just womankind in general. I loved it.

—Jill Scott

Girlfriend Getaway Ideas

Create a close-to-home adventure. Travel of any kind isn't mandatory for a truly wonderful girlfriends' escapade. Mix it up and go to a new restaurant or show you've been meaning to try out with your friends. Michelle once took a few of her closest female friends out for a night of Mexican food (Michelle's favorite) and then on to catch a Jill Scott concert in Washington, D.C.

Visit Manhattan, the capital of the world. If you *can* get out of town but it's too much of a burden for you and your pals to travel outside the states, New York City is a perfect alternative. Broadway shows, amazing eateries, and film festivals are the norm in this town filled to the brim with every form of culture imaginable. Not to mention Bergdorf, Saks, and the home offices of every major designer featured in *Vogue* are located there.

Now showing . . . at home. After becoming a mom Michelle reserved every Saturday morning for movies and lunch with friends and their kids. There's no end to what you can do to maintain, strengthen, and nurture lifelong bonds. Just do it. Channel your inner Michelle by arranging a soul-searching, eye-dabbing, all-girls film fest. Using Michelle as your guide, pick a few films that you know your inner circle will cherish for the laughter, love, and heart-wrenching dialogue. Here are five films Michelle would surely approve of.

- ***Pride and Prejudice* (2005), starring Keira Knightley and Matthew Macfadyen**

The 1813 Jane Austen book has been made and re-made into a film dozens of times, but none is so effortlessly stylish and delightfully moving as this most recent version. Knightley brings a mischievous, modern-day charm to the role of Elizabeth Bennett, while Macfadyen adds a more humble grace to the prideful Mr. Darcy. What could foster sisterhood among friends more than a film about five sisters in a mad rush for marriage? If one scene can make you believe in the power of love, it's Mr. Darcy's early morning declaration of love to Elizabeth in the middle of a cornfield with these words: "You have bewitched me body and soul and from this day we shall never part." Classic.

- *Mahogany* (1975), starring Diana Ross and Billy Dee Williams

The divine Ms. Ross is at her cinematic peak in this film and she uses each and every scene to wow her adoring audience as Tracy. With clothes, hair, and mile-high eyelashes that would make Carrie Bradshaw jealous, *Mahogany* is said to be one of Michelle's favorite films. You and your girls will understand why as you revel in Tracy's spirit as she rises from being an inner-city secretary to the world's top fashion model and an aspiring designer. You'll collectively swoon over the gallant attempts made by Billy Dee Williams's character to bring Tracy, his one true love, back home to Chicago. Of course your group will repeat in unison the oft-used phrase "Success means nothing without someone to share it with."

- *Thelma and Louise* (1991), starring Susan Sarandon and Geena Davis

This film gave the term "chick flick" an entirely different meaning when it hit theaters. Though a bit on the dreary side, the story of an Arkansas waitress and a housewife on the run after shooting a rapist is also inspirational, particularly when Thelma says, "You said you 'n' me was gonna get out of town and for once just really let our hair down. Well, darlin', look out, 'cause my hair is comin' down!" The two lead characters present the epitome of friendship to the end. This film also introduced the world to Brad Pitt. Enough said.

- *Claudine* (1974), **starring Diahann Carroll and James Earl Jones**

Another urban love story, but this time set in Harlem, featuring the flawless Diahann Carroll as a mother of six on welfare, struggling to make ends meet while still attempting to have a life of her own. When she does fall in love with a cheerful trash man, portrayed by Jones, there's no end to the comedy, heartache, and family dysfunction revealed. Still, the end is a happy one and the soundtrack, featuring Curtis Mayfield and Gladys Knight and the Pips, will keep you and your girls grooving for days.

- *Breakfast at Tiffany's* (1961), **starring Audrey Hepburn, George Peppard, and the entire Upper East Side of New York**

This iconic film proves why every woman should own a strand of pearls, oversized sunglasses, and a little black dress if she wants to succeed in the world. Holly Golightly is a pop culture icon, a resourceful and breezy heroine. Watch, bond, and learn.

Do not bring people in your life who weigh you down. And trust your instincts . . . good relationships feel good. They feel right. They don't hurt. They are not painful. That's not just with people you marry, but it's with the friends that you surround yourself with.

—MO

Good-bye to Yesterday

As wonderful as true friendships can be in your life, all aren't meant to last a lifetime. Once Barack became more and more visible on the political scene, Michelle was forced to make some tough choices on who to keep in and who to wean out of her inner circle. Friends she hadn't spoken to in years were coming out of the woodwork during Obama's rise to the White House, forcing Michelle to take a long hard look at the people she called friends.

While you might not be headed to the oval office like Michelle, it's never a bad idea to take stock of those around you. Remember that just as relationships with romantic partners can come to an end, so can friendships with girlfriends. If you continue to live a life that moves upward and forward you're bound to outgrow a few people who have been mainstays in your life. It can be exceptionally hard to leave people behind as you mature, but there may be instances where you'll have no choice. The key is understanding when the time is right to cut the ties that bind with a friendship that has served its purpose. Some people are truly only meant to be around for a season. Not recognizing that and not letting go when you should will only invite more friction, complications, and stress in your life.

Not sure if it's time to move on from a longtime sista friendship? Here are a few questions to help you find out.

• Do you enjoy talking about the same things? If you rarely laugh at the same things or haven't agreed on anything since the tenth grade, it may be time to take a break. Friendships are often based on common interests and passions but those can change through the years and so will you. So if the conversation with an old girlfriend now seems forced and stale, it may be time to slowly part ways.

• Does she greet your good news with less-than-enthused responses? Not every woman is jealous of you or what you have but let's face it, some are. If a good friend rarely rejoices at your exciting news about a new job, project, or accomplishment, it may be time to rethink your bond. A friend who can't sincerely share in your happiness isn't someone you need around.

• Does her friendship make you a better person? Friends should help to lift you up and make you better. Honestly ask yourself if certain friends cause more trouble than joy. Do they put you in compromising situations on a regular basis? Is the friendship one-way? If you're always the one making the calls to get together or just to keep in touch, your friend may have already figured out what you haven't. If they don't call or come by, they're just not that interested in being friends.

• Is it a negative friendship? Negative energy can impact you in many ways. Don't underestimate how much a friend who complains all the time can affect your outlook on life. If she's just going through a bad patch, hang in there with her. If it continues with no end in sight, save yourself, and walk away.

Making the Connection

Even if you've always been successful in making and keeping friends all of your life like Michelle, there are always new ones to be made and chances are you may find yourself in a situation where you'll *need* to make a new one along the way. A change of job or a move can call for the discovery of new friends and acquaintances. A relatively easy task for kids can be an incredibly daunting exercise for adults. As we mature, our tastes and interests become more defined, refined, and also a tad more narrow. Not exactly the best mind-set to integrate new people or practices into your life. But don't be discouraged. Getting to know new people at any point in your journey is just a matter of effort.

When Michelle moved to Washington, D.C., with her family after her husband was elected president in 2008, she was fortunate that several of her close Chicago friends, like Valerie Jarrett and Desiree Rogers, also joined her in the new neighborhood. However, many of her dear and valued friends were left behind. Of course, friendships can be nurtured from afar, but it's rarely the same when hundreds of miles separate you. Michelle hasn't missed a beat. She finds time to keep tabs on old pals while continuing to add local names to her Rolodex.

Go the Extra Mile:

Michelle stays in touch with her friends and so can you! Sign up for a free account with Skype and you can have face time with friends around the world.

If you find yourself having to start over in the friendship department, channel your inner Michelle and try a mixture of old and new methods to bring new faces into your life. It can begin with basic moves like chatting up the woman who lives next door or the woman under the dryer next to yours while at the beauty salon. Why not invite the woman who's always at the nail salon with you out to lunch? At your new job, try mingling after work with your coworkers. It may be hit-and-miss for a while, but eventually you'll click with someone. If you have children, bond with other mothers at the playground or while working on school committees. Sisterly bonds are a must while chaperoning school dances or organizing bake sales.

If you're willing to take it up a notch, join Facebook or Twitter. Those sites have many groups geared toward those who share a love of a favorite movie, book, or TV show. If she were to try Facebook, Michelle would no doubt be a major contributor to the *Sex and the City* fan page. The daily forums can introduce you to people with similar interests right in your own backyard or cubicle. The options are limitless for you to meet others online since there are so many social networking sites geared to particular interests and passions. There's even an online-based ministry for women called Girlfriends Pray that unites women all over the country through spiritual encouragement and support.

You can also use social networking to find out who from your old neighborhood is only a few degrees separated from someone in your new one. Ask them to make an introduction. You may even develop a lasting bond with a friend of a friend. Stranger things have happened.

Rule of Thumb No. 10: Strike Up a Conversation

If you often find yourself at a loss for words when meeting new people, take charge by creating a mental list of topics you enjoy conversing about freely and reference them when the situation arises. Here's where reading like Michelle comes in handy. Referring to the latest news headlines is a quick way of kicking off a hearty chat about the events of the day.

Or take another page from the book of Michelle by simply inquiring about a new friend's family or friends. Michelle employed this tactic while working in the private sector and continues to utilize it in her role at the White House. It's human nature that people appreciate any concern or interest shown in those close to them. And since most people have extended family somewhere, the opportunities to address countless topics are endless. Child care, health care, school zones, and baby showers are just a few of the subjects that may come up as a result of a question about someone's nearest and dearest.

The key to striking up a meaningful conversation with anyone is offering them a chance to see who you really are. In an effort to impress make sure not to go overboard by altering your true personality or by forcing a conversation that isn't happening naturally. Don't hesitate to share your opinions and thoughts on people, places, or events while giving equal time to your new potential friend's position.

In Michelle's role as First Lady, she's required to regularly meet and converse with new and unknown faces daily and she handles it with relative ease. Like most things, practice makes perfect. Even if you aren't in search of a new group of friends, make it a point to begin a conversation with someone new each month. It can be the woman who shares your morning commute or the girl who sits behind you in yoga class. Not only will you gain confidence from knowing you can talk to anyone at any time, you are bound to learn a thing or two along the way.

Chapter Four
Embrace the Beauty You Were Born With

We all have to make time for ourselves as women. That means getting our hair and nails done so we can feel good about ourselves.

—MO

*M*ichelle's striking good looks and polished presence took the mainstream beauty and fashion industries by storm, if not by surprise, in 2007. With her posture always upright, hair always whipped to perfection, and smooth brown skin always glowing, Michelle rarely failed to offer a stunning profile each time the cameras turned her way. Yet as effortless as Michelle's elegant, chic, and relatable look may appear to the untrained eye, rest assured that essential steps are continuously being taken by Michelle and her team to create the fabulous image she presents each and every time she's in public.

While the Chicago native had little choice but to intensify her focus on beauty, grooming, and upkeep as her husband gained political clout during the 2008 elections,

Michelle was no stranger to doing all she could to look her very best. As a child, even when money was low at the Robinson home Michelle researched and found alternative and inexpensive ways of highlighting her very best qualities. She simply wouldn't allow any nagging feelings of insecurity about her height, deep skin color, or tightly curled hair to seep into her mind or wreak havoc on her self-esteem. It mattered little to Michelle that popular magazines and television shows of the time rarely showcased or embraced women with physical qualities similar to her own.

Michelle's strong self-confidence allowed her to believe that what she had in both beauty and brains was more than enough. She was right. Adopt a like mind-set and follow in Michelle's footsteps by learning to embrace your own unique beauty while mastering a few tricks of the trade to enhance what you already have.

Michelle is an amazing beauty and a confident beauty and a real beauty. Obama is a lucky man.

—Will Smith

Beauty on a Budget

Like most teenage girls then and now, Michelle did all she could to appear perfectly groomed and immaculately dressed at all times during her high school years. She knew her long, lanky frame and above-average height would draw tons of additional attention her way.

With limited cash to spend on popular eighties staples like Bonne Bell lip balm or Maybelline black liquid eyeliner, Michelle routinely relied on good old common sense to enhance her "girl next door" looks. Each morning she'd slather on Vaseline to keep her lips shiny and moisturized and to keep her skin smooth, soft, and ash-free. In the makeshift bedroom she and her brother shared, divided by a large piece of cloth, Michelle finished her homework before performing her nightly beauty rituals of rolling her hair, showering and washing her face with a plain bar of Ivory soap. Blessed with wonderfully clear, even-toned skin, Michelle didn't have much use for heavy makeup or foundation during her teen years, a good thing given popular companies such as MAC and Make Up For Ever didn't exist yet and the makeup lines that were in existence hadn't quite recognized the need to formulate their products for minority skin. Popular eighties stars like Diana Ross, Janet Jackson, and Kim Fields (Tootie from *The Facts of Life*) would spend hundreds of dollars on custom-blended makeup to match their skin tones. A spotless face, shiny lips, and meticulously styled hair would have to do for young Michelle.

Michelle always walked with her head high and with her back straight. Many women her height would slouch down in an effort to appear shorter. Not Michelle; she wore her height with pride.
—One of Michelle's elementary school teachers

"Whip It" Like Michelle

Thankfully, the budding non-traditional beauty was indeed fortunate enough to have been born with a number of head-turning physical attributes all her own, including the thick shoulder-grazing hair that continues to frame her face today.

Until high school, Michelle's mother, Marian, assisted her daughter by straightening her textured hair weekly, while Michelle alternately wore it in a press-and-curl for special occasions such as church and school class pictures. Straightening African-American hair with a hot comb continues to be a long-standing tradition in many black homes, though not a particularly healthy (or fun) one since it involves applying searing heat to hair that is often fragile and weak.

As fate would have it, by the time she reached her senior year in high school, just in time for proms, dates, and graduation, eighteen-year-old Michelle was introduced by a friend to Michael "Rahni" Flowers, a popular Chicago hairstylist known for his magic fingers, especially with African-American tresses. At his posh midtown salon Van Cleef Hair Studio, Rahni embraced his new teenage client by explaining the exact nature of her curl pattern and how best to care for it. He also suggested her hair would benefit greatly from a chemical relaxer, which would give it more bounce, movement, and flexibility. A lasting quest for gorgeous, healthy hair was born that day for the future First Lady.

Rule of Thumb No. 11: Find the Best Look for You

When Michelle decided it was time to visit a true professional for her hair, she didn't have the luxury of Yelp or Google. Even if she had, odds are that common sense would have steered her in a more logical direction. When contemplating personal services that have to do with the you others notice first, seeing really is believing. Hair maintenance, eyebrow waxing, and major makeup applications are best carried out by someone you're confident in—based on seeing their finished work up close and personal, and on someone else. So when you notice a woman with similar features and love how she looks, don't be shy. Introduce yourself and genuinely compliment her style. She'll appreciate it. Then ask if she'd mind sharing the name of her stylist with you. Extreme flattery should cut through that nasty little habit some women have of not willingly sharing when asked about their dream team of beauty helpers.

Note to the reader: Don't be that woman. If you know of anything that could help a fellow female comrade in beauty need, share the wealth. Bad cosmetic karma can manifest itself in ill-timed ways. Remember, Michelle secured Rahni's A+ talents through a close family friend whose hair she loved.

Michelle likes to look elegant, classy, and self-assured and that includes her hair. She doesn't like a lot of fuss over it.
—Rahni Flowers, Michelle's longtime Chicago hairdresser

On Her Own

Michelle's beauty evolution got a huge assist from Rahni when he offered her step-by-step guidance on how to care for her tresses while she was in college at Princeton and law school at Harvard. His most valued gem of advice? If she ever needed to prolong her hair's frizz-free relaxed texture in between visits back home, all she needed was a soft brush to gently stretch the roots out after washing and voilà! This trick provided Michelle with two additional weeks of reduced frizz and manageable hair. She continued to absorb Rahni's healthy-hair wisdom like the dutiful schoolgirl she was, never hesitating to make a beeline for Rahni's chair each time she returned home to Chicago. Maintaining a great look is best left to the professionals.

Over time and with age, Michelle has altered her signature look ever so slightly but has never veered far from her traditional softly layered bob, with a few modifications in color and length. Her standing weekly hair appointment—she often met Rahni at his midtown studio at four A.M.—was a must and her simple, carefree hair choices looked great without burdening her with maintenance time. No wonder she has carried them through to this day. When it comes to the First Lady's crown of glory, the woman who loves mental challenges of all sorts accepts the tried-and-true mantra "Better to be safe than sorry."

While Rahni declined Michelle's offer to join her in Washington in 2008, he till tends to her tresses when she visits her hometown. "She wanted me to come with her to D.C. but I couldn't leave my life and clients in Chicago," says Rahni. In true Rahni style, he made sure the hairdresser who currently coifs Michelle's tresses received all his tips, suggestions, and products to keep her hair looking good.

Rahni's Treasure Trove of Products for Michelle-like Tresses

Rahni Flowers created his trademark Double Deep special custom conditioning blend of four different products just for Michelle when her constant traveling and daily heat styling began causing slight damage to her hair during the presidential campaign. His secret mixture of exotic oils (grape-seed oil is one) became such a hit that Flowers now offers it to all of his clients. But you must make a trip to the Windy City if you want to sample Rahni's special concoction. If you're looking to spruce up your locks, consider the below products as if Michelle herself recommended them to you. They can be purchased in most beauty shops or ordered online.

- *Infusium 23 (brown label)* Rahni recommends this lightweight, moisturizing leave-in treatment be applied to all hair types prior to use of heat and styling.
- *Body Bounce by Vitale* Rahni loves to use this moisturizing cream for Michelle's curly styles by applying it with his fingers to each section of her hair just after blow-drying. Body Bounce helps curls last longer and hair look fuller.
- *Lottabody setting lotion* Rahni recommends using a small dab of setting lotion (often mixed with Body Bounce) to achieve a longer-lasting roller-set style. The amount used depends on the length and style of your hair.
- *Control Paste by Aveda* Rahni loves this product for taming pesky flyaways and for smoothing the edges of hair, which frizz quickly. The formula doesn't rob moisture from the hair or flake, two things Rahni and Michelle both hate.
- *Shine Define by Sebastian* Rahni spritzed this on Michelle, Sasha, and Malia's hair the morning of the inauguration. This lightweight finishing spray provides soft hold and shine even in rain, sleet, or snow.

Healthy Hair Commandments

If limited finances are preventing you from visiting a professional stylist as often as you'd like, healthy hair is still yours
to have with a little work. Rahni offers his own special com-
mandments for the do-it-yourself diva.

Commandment No. 1

Thou shalt never over-process your hair by applying relax-
ers and perms too closely together. Always apply chemicals
to the new growth only and make sure to leave some of
your natural curl pattern intact by avoiding straightening
to the point of compromising the strength of the hair.

Commandment No. 2

Thou shalt not overuse any hairstyling product, including
shampoos and conditioners. Follow the product's instructions for usage—they put them there for a reason. Overuse will only cause your hair to go flat with product
buildup, which also prevents conditioners from doing
their job of penetrating the cuticle.

Commandment No. 3

Thou shalt not abuse holding sprays that contain alcohol,
particularly if you have chemically processed hair. Alcohol
dries the hair, which can lead to damage and ultimately
breakage.

Everyone's hair reacts differently to products and styling, so finding the right cocktail of products for your hair
may take some trial and error. Ask your stylist for recom-
mendations, and take note of the products he or she uses
when you visit the salon.

The Tricky Politics of Additional Hair

Michelle has managed to keep her free-flowing mane in tip-top shape with Rahni's help and, even more amazingly, while enduring the endless demands of official White House portraits, magazine shoots, and international travel. But during times when additional follicle support is not just desired but required, Michelle doesn't resist the use of wigs, hair pieces, and other accessories for enhancement, and for good reason. Within hours of any public appearance she makes, high-resolution photos are sure to appear across every media outlet in the world, inviting intense scrutiny of the severest kind on her every textured strand. Translation: Bad hair days simply aren't allowed.

Of course Michelle isn't the first First Lady to partake in a little "hair aid." Jackie Kennedy Onassis fully appreciated the art of attaching faux hair falls, buns, and ponytails to her medium-length brunette mane and even had special pieces custom-made for certain White House occasions.

I am not my hair.

—India Arie, Grammy-award-winning musician

Though women of all races routinely attach faux hair to their tresses for overall physical enhancement and have done so for decades, African-American women usually receive the majority of the focus and the bulk of the criticism for embracing the habit. Somewhere along the line, women of color have been unfairly burdened with the responsibility of "keeping it real" while today's most revered beauties of all races, including Kim Kardashian, Jessica Simpson (who even touts her own faux-hair line), and Jennifer Lopez make no bones about their regular use of hair extensions. Why the glaring double standard?

Who knows, but rest assured that when Michelle feels her precious locks need a break from the heat, wind, and rain of life, or when she needs a bit more fullness to her layered bob, she gives little thought to the short-sighted opinions of others. Michelle knows a few tracks of Indian remy, or for that matter an entire head of extensions, is no more a barometer of her character or "realness" than a full set of dental veneers or colored contacts would be.

Stick with whatever floats your boat when it's time to revamp or enhance your looks. Remember the golden rule of hair: Whether you grew it, bought it, or clipped it on, if it looks good and makes you feel good, who cares?

A Few Good Strands

If the word "extensions" makes you think of stick-straight down-to-your-back hair that you can't touch, then you have been missing out on the advancements hair companies have made in the past ten years. Michelle is known to prefer relatively short and layered wigs and hair units for various public occasions. Wigs and hair units, which can be snapped on and off, are easily removed at night as opposed to tracks sewn in for extensions or weaves. So remember, whether your hair is long, medium, or short, any style can be complemented with the help of a few extra strands. Here's a quick primer on some of the great options out there.

> **Wigs ($50 and up; no installation time)** Michelle often wears wigs to alter her look quickly and to avoid the restrictions posed by a sewn-in weave. On many

Go the Extra Mile:

The right hairstyle can change your whole look for the better. If you're considering a new do, do your homework. *People* Style Watch, *Essence*, and *InStyle* all have Web sites that will Photoshop a picture of you to show how you would look with a variety of hairstyles and colors. Be real about the hair you currently have on your head. If your tresses are coarse and tightly curled, odds are installing a pack of European silky straight hair for your weave won't be very believable. Or if you have the lovely skin tone of models Alec Wek and Naomi Campbell, understand the delightful blond hair color you just love on Beyoncé probably won't be a good look for you. Your revamping process should be all about positively building on what you already have.

occasions, such as her trip to South Africa in 2011, Michelle wore a stylishly cropped wig to look neatly groomed in the midst of the blinding heat of that country and also to avoid the damaging impact of daily heat styling on her own hair. This also gave her more free time to spend with the people of the country she had dreamed of visiting for so long and not in the chairs of her hair and make-up people. If you plan on channeling your inner Michelle, higher-end companies like Extensions Plus in California specialize in producing well-made, long-lasting hairpieces that look exactly like your own hair. You can be sure Oprah Winfrey, Beyoncé, and Serena Williams regularly sport these custom-made hair units. Keep in a mind a hairpiece similar to the ones those ladies wear may set you back a few thousand dollars. Serena likes to buy five to ten hair units at a time. Save up.

Weaves ($300–500; 4–7 hours for installation) Weaves have also grown in popularity by leaps and bounds since the traditional sewn-in method was developed in the late sixties. Today weaves can be achieved and installed in various methods that allow for greater freedom and flexibility. They provide a certain amount of versatility for women and last for a few months. The list of weave-wearing divas is literally endless in Hollywood. Popular starlets Rihanna, Sandra Bullock, and Britney Spears have all employed some type of hair extension.

Shrink Links ($800–2,000; about 4 hours for installation) One of the latest additions to advanced hair technology, this technique involves taking a small section of hair and applying a specially made glue to attach new hair through a slender cylinder. This eliminates the bulk of tracks and allows you to remain worry-free when a large gust of wind blows by without warning. Jennifer Aniston and Beyoncé have both used this method, which lasts a few weeks. Warning: This method can also cause damage once removed. So be sure to hire a trained professional.

Hair skin wefts ($150 per weft; no time needed to apply) These cute temporary pieces have sections of hair attached to peel-off adhesive strips that lie flat against the scalp for a very natural look. The strips can be reused several times and they stay put through several shampoos. Perfect for special occasions or date night to give quick fullness and volume. Celebs such as La La, Kelly Rowland, and Ciara have tried this method. **Traditional braided weave ($200–700 plus the cost of the hair; 4–5 hours for installation)** This old standby remains the most popular method of adding additional hair and the most healthy, as braiding encourages growth and allows your own hair rest from heat and styling completely. It requires a professional to braid your hair and then sew the purchased hair into your braids.

Rule of Thumb No. 12: Keep It Simple

Michelle found it much easier to navigate the basics of hair care before ever wandering into the massive maze that is skin care and makeup. Thankfully for Michelle, her flawless skin gave her an extended pass from wearing foundation or heavy makeup of any kind. Instead, as she entered law school and headed into the workforce, Michelle took baby steps in her use of products designed to add color and detail. Adhering to her usual mantra of less is more, Michelle's regular makeup uniform prior to taking center stage a few years ago simply included a tinted lip gloss, a quick pat of MAC pressed powder to eliminate shine, and a touch of eyeliner and mascara for definition. She revamped her casual approach to cosmetics through the years, causing many to raise an eyebrow when she became the first and only First Lady to employ a full-time makeup artist.

Go the Extra Mile:
Michelle had it right from the start. Less really *is* more. Take some time to reevaluate your makeup bag. Dump anything you haven't been using and make sure you have what it takes to create an everyday look and a day-to-night look—that's really all you need.

Michelle Obama's beauty is a simple beauty, the very best kind.
—Sidney Poitier, Oscar winner

Take Care of Your Canvas

You won't have much luck following Michelle's lead on simple makeup if you haven't yet adopted a successful skin-care regime. Regardless of your age, any woman hoping to move gracefully into her later years should develop a skin-care plan as soon as she begins her first full-time job. Though there was a time when Michelle used plain soap to clean her face, she now prefers a creamy cleanser from Clinique to clear away the day's residue. She then applies a Clinique moisturizer best suited for her dry-to-normal skin and finishes up with a hydrating eye balm.

One of Michelle's regular makeup artists, Ingrid Grimes-Myles, says she rarely has to discuss with her famous client the importance of good skin care or the many benefits of drinking tons of water daily.

She's a statuesque woman with beautiful skin. She makes my job very easy.

—Ingrid Grimes-Myles

Top Tips for Clear Skin

While we can't all be blessed with Michelle's great genes, here are some practices Grimes-Myles suggests that will help any woman get her skin situation under control.

1. Your mother was right. Drinking water is the answer to nearly all your health woes. Not only does it keep your skin moist, it keeps your entire system lubricated. To make your water more interesting, add lemon or cucumber slices, or test the many low-calorie powder mixes available for your H_2O. Your skin will thank you.

2. Use lukewarm water to cleanse your skin twice a day. Water that is too hot or cold can do damage. Find a cleanser based on your skin type (dry, normal, oily, or combination) and no matter how late you come in from a glorious night out, wash your face. Use a quick wipe or wet a warm towel,

but do wash off the oils and makeup of the day. Failure to do so will surely result in impurities surfacing in not-so-pleasant ways.

3. Never use soap. As Michelle learned after leaving high school, soap is way too drying even for oily skin and is best used below the neck, if at all. If possible use a cream or gel cleanser for the skin on your face and a liquid wash for your body to ensure your skin is well moisturized. Michelle loves creamy cleansers and fragrant bath oils to keep a nice sheen. Jada and Will Smith have given Michelle an array of lotions, creams, and body washes from the Carol's Daughter collection. Michelle is said to adore these products, which tout all-natural oils and ingredients, for both herself and her girls. The Smiths have partial ownership in the line.

4. Use sunscreen every day. Simplify your daily regime by finding a combination sunscreen and moisturizer and apply generously before leaving the house. If you have darker skin like Michelle, test the sunscreen formulation before purchasing to make sure it doesn't leave a chalky cast on your skin after application. If you are outside for most of the day, carry a travel-size tube with you to reapply as needed.

5. Get a good night's sleep and engage in some form of exercise daily. Lack of sleep can cause wrinkles to form below your eyes and lack of exercise can cause your skin to sag. Neither is very desirable.

I began to prioritize exercise because I realized that my happiness was tied to how I feel about myself.

—MO

Give Good Face

Once you feel comfortable with your skin-care choices, it's time to bring your makeup game up to par. You may ask, is makeup really required? Of course, many women don't think so and resist the use of any makeup. Some feel it's a little too time-consuming while others seem convinced it will add nothing to their already natural beauty. All valid points of course, but as a rule most makeup artists insist that even if you have been blessed with the most beautiful skin in town, a little gloss, eyeliner, and powder can do wonders for your overall presentation. Not to mention the fact that foundation also protects skin from the damaging impact harsh climate changes can cause. "It's all about being polished," says Schuron Womack, a Los Angeles–based MAC makeup artist who works with Hollywood actresses like Stacey Dash, Regina King, and Tracee Ellis Ross. "Just a little powder to reduce shine, a bit of eyeliner to wake up your eyes, and some lip gloss to bring attention to the center of your face is such an easy way to look together and professional in a short period of time," says Womack.

Michelle's not a performer. Her look is that of a professional woman who has to look good on the job and look good when she's with her kids.

—Ingrid Grimes-Myles

Doing More with Less

Michelle's favorite makeup looks have rarely strayed from the classic and the timeless through the years. As Barack began to show political clout, Michelle was forced to step up her makeup moves for photo shoots and television appearances. She met makeup artist Ingrid Grimes-Myles while appearing on a local Chicago news show and adored the fact that Grimes-Myles's application techniques allowed her skin to breathe and show through. Grimes-Myles began working with her for special events and now works regularly with the First Lady in Washington. She spilled on Michelle's famed features for us.

Face. On days she has to make public and television appearances, Michelle relies on a cream foundation topped with powder to maintain longevity and keep shine at bay. To give her face definition and polish, Michelle's makeup artist uses contour powder instead of blush. She applies a powder (one shade darker than Michelle's skin tone) along the base of her cheekbones. Contouring gives the First Lady a nice chiseled bone structure. Using that same dark powder along the sides of your jawline can also be used to slim a double chin or narrow a chubby face if required.

Eyes. Michelle prefers muted earth tones on her lids for day events, and for evening occasions she loves a dramatic gray, smoky eye, paired with a few added lashes at the corners of her eyes. Kohl-black eyeliner is applied on both her upper lids and waterline, while jet-black mascara completes the look.

Eyebrows. The First Lady took some heat for the "angry" look of her eyebrows during the 2008 presidential campaign.

Michelle's natural arch is rather high, which can result in a constant quizzical look. To offset that, Grimes now makes sure to shape Michelle's eyebrows so they start at the beginning of her eye and arch at the end of the iris. This minor tweak made a world of difference.

Lips. Michelle rarely wears lipstick, considering it too heavy and aging. Instead, she prefers pretty-in-pink lip glosses and also uses a mixture of moisturizing glosses from MAC for just the right shade. Her trick for keeping glosses inside the lip line is a pencil lip liner in the same shade used all over the lips and then topped with lip gloss. The pencil creates a stain effect.

Give Good Everyday Face

With Michelle's mantra of "Less is more" in mind, create your own makeup routine that gives you a stunning appearance without making you resemble a circus runaway. Schuron Womack offers these guidelines for looking fabulous with minimal effort.

- Start with a good moisturizer, and then use a powder foundation to get quick and easy coverage for your skin while reducing shine throughout the day.
- Try a neutral-tone eye shadow that covers your entire eyelid for a fresh everyday look. Beige and bronze colors work well on most complexions.
- Line your eyes with either a brown or black waterproof eyeliner to give them definition and personality. For extra staying power, go over

your pencil liner with a liquid gel or powdered eye shadow to avoid the dreaded raccoon look after a long day.

- To define your eyebrows, use a brown powder eye shadow or pencil. A clear brow gel will keep them neat and in place. Always keep your brows free of strays and shaped as they provide structure to your face.
- A few coats of black or brown mascara on your lashes finishes the look of your eyes. For a fuller look, curl them first.
- Add a touch of blush to brighten up your face and give it dimension. Pink and mauves are perfect for daytime.
- Top off your look with a swipe of gloss in pink, Michelle's color of choice, or a nude shade that pulls your entire look together.

Watch and Learn

For those of us who don't have a makeup artist at our beck and call, there are other effective steps you can take to ensure you find the right look that highlights your natural beauty. It may have taken some time for Michelle to master her own makeup game, but she didn't have access to the multiple media outlets now available to guide anyone through the ins and outs of the wonderful world of beauty. Learning how to apply makeup that enhances your natural beauty instead of masking it can be as simple as turning your computer on.

Whether you're interested in learning how to tightline your eyes, find the right bronzer, or cover acne scars with concealer, the videos created by many well-known makeup artists on YouTube and their own personal blogs can be the answer you're looking for. Bookmark these Internet makeup gurus' sites and videos and you'll always be up on the most updated looks.

Tiffany D: Check out this self-taught makeup artist's frequent updates on the latest brands and products. (makeupbytiffanyd.blogspot.com)

SimplYounique: Kerry's site aims to inspire and motivate a different type of beauty through detailed hair and makeup advice for all skin tones and hair textures. (www.youtube.com/simplyounique)

Makeup Geek: Marlena offers a rundown of the most popular products as well as no-nonsense re-views on the bestselling beauty items on the market. (www.makeupgeek.com)

Scandalous Beauty: Erin's tutorials on face contour-ing, shading, and foundation application are super-easy to follow and fun to watch. (www.scandalous beautyonline.com)

Mikki Bey: This makeup artist enjoys mixing useful makeup advice with lessons on love and life. (mikkibey .blogspot.com)

Avoiding Beauty Blunders

Discovering what products and techniques work for you can be a tedious process, so think of it as a learning experience. You can have fun, learn a little bit, and like what you see in the mirror along the way. Most of the errors are in the details and even makeup mavens have made a few of them from time to time. Here are a few you should always avoid.

Using the wrong shade of foundation or concealer. Foundation is supposed to match the tone of skin as it appears in natural light. When purchasing, hold the color up to your forearm; the area underneath the wrist is where many cosmetologists say the skin most closely resembles the face. When applying to your face, blend, blend, blend beyond the jaw into your neck so the color transitions into your skin's natural shade. No masks, please.

Rushing the application. Makeup is like a house: If the foundation is shaky, the rest of the look will fall apart. Applying makeup can be time-consuming, but if you take shortcuts, it will show. It will also show if you apply it during your daily commute—you know who you are. Stop that bad habit! Use moisturizer and primer in separate layers and allow a few minutes for your skin to absorb one before applying the other. Both primer and moisturizer act as a barrier between your skin and your arsenal of cosmetics.

Sleeping in your makeup. This is a big no-no because it's a breeding ground for bacteria. Don't go to bed without washing your face—ever. The same basic care is also needed for your tools. Wash your brushes once a week with a gentle soap or shampoo, rinse thoroughly, wrap in a towel, and lay them flat to dry. And remember, only use your own set of makeup brushes. Friends don't share bacteria with friends.

Ignoring the shelf life. Most products expire and makeup is not an exception. After a certain time, products become less effective, harbor germs, and work against your desired look. Cosmetics aren't legally required to post an expiration date so you'll have to keep tabs. As a rule, mascara is good for two to three months; eyeliner, face cream, and eye cream last about six months; and foundation can be used for up to a year. Lipstick, gloss, blush, and shadow can last for up to three years.

Rocking the same makeup at thirty that you wore at sixteen. It's easy to become comfortable with a look that's served you well in the past. But your makeup should be a reflection of who you are today. Take a chance on colors as bold and as bright as your personality, and leave the dark lip liner, frosted shadow on the entire lid, and shimmery pink lipsticks in the eighties where they belong.

Overkill. Just because you've decided to experiment with bright colors doesn't mean you should wear them all at the same time. Leave that practice to Lady Gaga or Nicki Minaj. It's all about balance, so play up one feature at a time. Dramatic eye color and faux lashes mean your lips should have sheer, subtle color. Your features shouldn't compete with each other for the spotlight.

Get Your Workout On

Just one look at Michelle's svelte frame and you know this is a woman who rarely ever skips her gym appointments. After the birth of her first daughter, Malia, Michelle began rising before dawn to get at least thirty minutes to an hour's worth of exercise. As life became more overwhelming for Michelle, she didn't use her tightly packed schedule as an excuse to reduce her time at the gym. Instead she did exactly the opposite. "She truly committed herself to the importance of health and fitness," Cornell McClellan, Michelle's longtime Chicago trainer, explains.

Michelle understood that staying physically fit provided her with more than just a stunning silhouette. Summoning the discipline to meet her trainer at five A.M. three times a week, Michelle proved she was the one and only keeper of her own health, happiness, and future.

For the last fifteen years the core of Michelle's workout plan has been a weight-training routine made up of compound movements that work multiple muscle groups. In one workout, Michelle might do one set of fifteen to twenty reps each of lunges, bench presses, hip raises, and rows, all without taking a break. She also mixes in short bouts of intense cardio. For a bigger challenge (and we know how much Michelle loves those) her trainer puts her through an even greater total-body workout that combines jump-roping, kickboxing, and body-weight calisthenics, all done at a pace that skyrockets fitness levels and burns tons of calories.

Tone Up

It's hard to pinpoint the exact occasion or moment Michelle's well-toned yet feminine arms made their debut and became the talk of the town. Maybe it was the front-and-center positioning they received on her highly celebrated 2009 *Vogue* cover, or maybe it was an appearance at a state dinner early in the Obama administration that brought those arms into the national dialogue and spotlight. Either way, per usual, Michelle has given women yet another goal to reach for. Think it's impossible to get those defined shoulders, strong biceps, and firm triceps of your dreams without putting hours upon hours in at the gym? Think again.

Besides her intense routine of weight training and cardio, Michelle ends her workout with what is referred to as an arm-shaping superset. "What's supersetting?" you may ask. It's a simple exercise protocol that saves you time, increases intensity, and helps you break through any weight-loss plateau you may have hit. Do bear in mind that supersetting is an advanced training protocol in which you do two or three exercises one after another—with no rest in between. The exercises can be for the same muscle group or two different muscle groups.

Michelle's upper-arm exercises consist of triceps push-downs and hammer curls. If you're looking to tone up, try this nine-minute superset three days a week (you'll need a pair of two-or-three-pound dumbbells and resistance bands). If you stay true to this routine you should notice a difference in less than a month.

- Perform a set of ten to fifteen triceps push-downs using a set of resistance bands. Repeat. For visual instructions, check out the female model videos on BodyBuilding.com.
- Without resting, perform a set of six hammer curls using dumbbells or resistance bands: Hold two dumbbells at your sides, palms facing in,

arms straight. Keeping your elbows at your sides, raise one dumbbell until your thumb faces your shoulder. Lower to the original position and repeat with your other arm.

- Rest for one minute, then repeat the entire process again for two or three sets of both exercises.

No Gym, No Problem

While the benefits of regular exercise go way beyond your skin, deterrents like money and time keep many women from pursuing self-improvement and better health. Don't let them! Even if you don't have Michelle's regular access to a personal trainer, never fear; here are a number of easy and effective exercises you can try anytime and anyplace to stay glowing, fit, and feeling good.

Walking

If you have stairs at home, use them! Instead of waiting for the elevator at work, take the stairs. If you take the bus or the train, get off a few stops ahead of your final destination and walk the rest of the way. Get your friends, kids, or dog and walk whenever possible but at least thirty minutes a day. It's simple, easy, and completely free!

Jumping Jacks

This calisthenic exercise will work out your shoulders, back, thighs, and calves. Start in a standing position with your feet together and your arms relaxed by your sides. Jump your feet apart so they are wider than your shoulders while at the same time raising your arms out to the sides until your hands are over your head. Then jump back into starting position. Get five sets of jumping jacks in while you're doing the laundry, or if you're brave, while waiting for the bus.

Leg Lifts

This exercise can be done while sitting in a chair at your desk. Sit upright in the chair while lifting your legs until they are parallel to the floor. Lower your legs slowly and stop three inches off the floor. Hold your legs steady for about two seconds and then come back up to your original position. Aim for five sets of leg lifts and you'll feel the results.

Squats

Knowing how to do squats properly can firm up your butt and legs rapidly. Stand with your legs apart in line with your shoulders while keeping your toes, hips, and knees in a straight line. Slowly lower your body as if you were going to sit down in a chair, bending your knees, and facing forward. Hold the position for two seconds and return to the starting position. Repeat ten to fifteen times for a seriously intense workout in the comfort of your living room with the television on.

Dancing

Dancing gives you flexibility, strength, endurance, and an overall sense of well-being, all from just switching on your favorite musical jams and moving. Michelle loves to exercise to upbeat tracks by Beyoncé and old-school jams by LL Cool J. Just half an hour (that's only seven songs) of fast-paced dancing burns upwards of 190 calories.

Go the Extra Mile:

Get a pedometer! For less than twenty dollars, you'll have an everyday exercise measurer and motivator. The U.S. surgeon general recommends a daily target of 10,000 steps a day. A 2004 study showed that the average American woman takes only about 5,200 steps a day. Get that number up and the benefits include increases in muscle strength and endurance, a decrease in blood pressure, and elevation of mood. Once you get started, it's addictive to see how you can get those steps in. Bonus points if you get one for a friend too and work on it together.

There's little question of whether looking good on the outside can do wonders for your inner confidence, but never neglect the part of your health that others can't see. Pay attention to your body and make note of any changes or aches and pains that linger or intensify over time. Michelle watched her father suffer with MS for years and one of her close college girlfriends succumb to cancer. Both made her über-vigilant about healthy living, including making regular visits to her doctors for yearly exams. Do your research and learn the tests required for your age group and lifestyle.

Chapter Five
Fashion-Forward

For me fashion is fun, and it's supposed to help you feel good about yourself. I think that's what all women should focus on: what makes them happy, and feeling comfortable and beautiful. I wear what I love. Sometimes people love it, sometimes they don't. I'm fine with it.

—MO

*M*ichelle's transformation into a fashion icon wasn't planned. Though she's effortlessly morphed into the role of trendsetter and style maven, it wasn't a role she actively sought. For the majority of Michelle's adult life she wore clothes that conveyed a certain sense of maturity, detail, and professionalism. She grew up without extra money to spend on Jordache jeans and after focusing on school moved right on to a job where her main goal was to look professional.

As a working mother, she needed looks that could take her from work to after-school events with ease. She frequented stores like Ann Taylor, Casual Corner, and Talbots for sharp signature suits and pieces that communicated her intelligence and desire to succeed on every level. But Barack's rise to presidential candidate and beyond forced her into the spotlight, which meant a big change for her image. When you get a promotion, have a new beau, or have any other need or desire for a change in your style, you can use the same tips to make over your look.

> Michelle is like many women who grew into her style and vision of fashion over time and as she got older. It's a rare woman that knows exactly what makes her look best from day one. Learning and developing a style takes time and thought. She had to get there.
> —Bethann Hardison, editor at large of Italian *Vogue*

Michelle did, over time, find her perfect fashion footing, and so can you with a bit of effort, research, and patience. Just as Michelle gradually grew into truly appreciating the clothing that best fit her body shape, taste, and work environment, so will you. It may be an extended period of trial and error for some, while others may find a style that fits their groove in no time. Wherever you fall in the search for your true fashion self, try not to let the limitless options offered by the world of style overwhelm you. Enjoy the process of learning more about what makes you unique both inside and out. Just like Michelle.

Be Stylish

To become a stylish woman you must first understand what being stylish means. It doesn't mean thoughtlessly following trends, designers, or hot names. Style is about individuality, your character, your mood, and even your dreams. Just like Michelle, a stylish woman chooses clothes that fit her body and her personality.

Learn. To be a grounded woman of style, you must learn the basics of choosing what's right for you. Oddly enough, that may require watching others to see how they put together outfits that look amazing on them. Skim international issues of *Vogue* and *Bazaar*, which tend to offer more fashion and less celebrity between their pages. Identify women who always look put together, and ask them their favorite places to shop. Fashionistas love it when their looks are admired and will be more than happy to share their tips.

Revise. Examine your current wardrobe. What's working? What no longer serves a purpose for you? Think about where you want to head in your fashion life and then swap or donate all the clothes that aren't going to help you get there. In this economy, everything needs recycling. Hard time cutting ties with clothes you love? Ask a trusted stylish friend for help evaluating what stays and goes, and to unwrap your hand from that shapeless sweater you have a sentimental attachment to.

Play it safe. Unsure about what combinations of colors work for your skin tone and taste? Stick with black and white, gray, and white, and monochromatic combinations. They call them classic for a reason. As you continue to build your wardrobe, decide what colors and styles work best for the look you want to create.

Experiment. Try different tones and textures in clothes that make you feel comfortable. A soft silk cream blouse against twill pants goes from day to night with the right earrings. A chunky knit sweater with dark skinny jeans is perfect for staying in, but with a kitten heel it can be great for a dinner date. Use your clothes, makeup, and haircut to allow your outer image to reflect the inner you.

Style for Success

As Michelle transitioned to strict office attire and beyond, she consistently purchased a few high-quality pieces that would help her move seamlessly from work to business dinners or events with the kids. Relatively safe pantsuits and structured suits in traditionally accepted business colors were her tried-and-true uniforms of choice. Michelle would later be motivated to take a different approach regarding her fashion choices, but you can start right now.

Even if your current place of employment requires you to showcase a formal demeanor through your clothes, remember you can still take a few chances with your look. Forget what you've heard; *accessories* are a girl's best friend, so brighten up your dark gray suits with a light blue or teal silk scarf or a pair of spectator shoes. An amazing pair of shoes can spice up the life of any mundane outfit. A well-made textured black leather bag along with a stylish and slightly chunky silver cuff can give your suits a modern, hip vibe. A pair of thin, medium-size hoop earrings and a beautiful peridot or blue topaz necklace can give your entire wardrobe a spotlight. Of course, please be sure your makeup and hair are on point as well. Flawless from head to toe means exactly that.

"People find Michelle and her clothes so interesting because there's a generation who've never experienced a First

Lady who enjoys fashion as much as Michelle does," explains Robin Givhan, *Newsweek* and the Daily Beast special correspondent for style and culture. "Hillary Clinton, Barbara Bush, and Laura Bush all had an uncomfortable relationship with style and a real disconnect and disinterest for the fashion industry as a whole. Michelle embraced the reality that fashion plays a major role in shaping how others see you."

Shoes Every Woman Should Own

With a size 12 foot, Michelle was forced to buy shoes with hefty price tags, if only because higher-end designers provided her with more options. Ladies' shoe sizes beyond size 10 can be tough to find, so Michelle found herself doing major research on shops that offered the most well-rounded selection of shoes and a vast variety of styles to suit her taste. No woman, including Michelle, wants to be limited in her choice of footwear. Take a tip from Michelle and make sure your closet features the five styles of shoe every woman needs to support a diverse and fashionable wardrobe.

High-heel stilettos. Every woman should own at least one pair of shoes that makes her feel sexy, slim, and tall. Michelle already has height in the bag, but a pair of gorgeous pumps by Manolo Blahnik or a lower-price line like Via Spiga can elongate your legs and give you a more defined, long, and lean silhouette. Michelle breaks her pairs out for special occasions, like the gunmetal sling-backs she wore to meet Kate Middleton.

Kitten-heel pumps. Michelle loves few things more than her signature kitten-heel pumps by designer Jimmy Choo. She also favors them to avoid towering over most people, including Barack. American women have been thanking her for bringing back a style that is both conservative and sexy. For you, a kitten heel can help you look stylish and chic in comfort.

A pair of tall black or brown boots. Every woman needs a pair of well-made leather boots to add personality and flair to her winter outfits. Boots have become even more versatile over the last few years, allowing you to wear them all year long and with a variety of outfits and styles. Purchase the highest-quality pair you can and have them for years to come. Michelle ordered a custom pair from renowned French shoemaker Robert Clergerie, who has previously made footwear for Madonna, Bianca Jagger, and Carla Bruni-Sarkozy.

Leather flats. Michelle loves her flats for the same reasons she adores her kitten-heel pumps. A nice pair of flats can offer you flexibility to stand or move around on your feet for hours on end in comfort. Both Michelle and Carla Bruni-Sarkozy finished off their outfits with flats for their first meeting, showing great fashion sense. A strappy pair of flat sandals and a simple pair of ballet flats—à la Audrey Hepburn—both make great wardrobe enhancers.

A sturdy pair of sneakers. Michelle constantly preaches the rewards of exercise and has been photographed wearing a unique and colorful variety of sneaker styles since moving to her White House address. From Keds to Converse high-tops, Michelle has rocked them all, whether working alongside students or at the World Series, and so should you.

Closet Staples

VH1 *Styled By June* star and celebrity stylist June Ambrose developed an impressive résumé by styling the big names of the music world. Ambrose may dress the icons of music, but she admits being a fan of Michelle's and closely follows the First Lady's evolution in fashion. For her own style, the New York native is the epitome of sleek and chic when she hits the streets of her hometown. Known for her Birkin bags, turbans, and oversize sunglasses, Ambrose shares the First Lady's penchant for a little J.Crew and JCPenney mixed in with high-end couture. Like Michelle, June also loves to add gemstone pendants and brightly hued scarves to give her outfits a dash of color and personality. Ambrose also understands Michelle's no-nonsense attitude toward fashion and the importance of tried-and-true closet staples.

No matter her job or budget, a lady should always have a few key pieces in her wardrobe to fall back on when she needs to look her best. Keep in mind these are just the basics, and just as Michelle discovered on her fashion journey, you too can continue to expand your choices over time by adding less severe and far more unique pieces to your wardrobe list. But as with all things, you must crawl before you can walk, so start with a solid fashion foundation before taking that leap to the next level. Michelle certainly did. Check your closet and make sure it includes each of the following:

A trench coat. It never goes out of style and always looks sophisticated. Invest in a high-quality piece to wear for the ages. For a touch of Michelle, be daring and try a trench coat that's made of leather or one that comes in an eye-catching moss green or cobalt blue. Put your own spin on what's expected.

A cardigan sweater. This is a quick and stylish way to dress any outfit up or down. Stock up on these in classic and statement-making colors, and consider a few with decorative buttons and other details. Michelle is a big fan of this musthave. On a visit to *The Tonight Show* in October of 2008, she wore a honey-colored J.Crew crystal-button cardigan over a silk tank top and a gold pencil skirt. In Grant Park in Chicago on election night in November of 2008, Michelle paired a black and red Narciso Rodriguez dress with a black cashmere cardigan by Azzedine Alaïa.

A tailored blazer. Thrown over jeans or a suit, this makes for an effortlessly dapper first date. Before she entered the public eye, Michelle had closets full of blazers that she used for her work in corporate America and wore whenever she needed to impress.

A little black or navy dress. Audrey Hepburn had one and so should you. The famous black dress she wore nearly fifty years ago in the iconic film *Breakfast at Tiffany's* sold for over $410,000 in 2006, and the use you will get out of this closet staple is priceless. Michelle usually applies her own special touch to the little black dress, and so can you. Play with texture and color when donning this classic piece. On the night her husband won the Democratic nomination in 2008, Michelle dazzled in a deep-purple Maria Pinto dress, accented by a black patent-leather Azzedine Alaïa belt and pearls.

A piece with a wonderful story. "Clothes either have a story or they should tell one," Ambrose says. Snag a favorite blouse during your weekend in Miami or a beautiful brooch or pendant while on vacation in the Bahamas. Those items will not only keep you stylishly chic, but they will also remind you of good times. That's a two-for-one deal. Michelle often wears a tiny diamond peace symbol that also features a tag that says "hope." A good friend gave her the Lena Wald piece shortly after Barack announced he was running for president. "Hope" was Barack's campaign slogan.

I never want to be a woman viewed as overly concerned with the way she looks. As a woman I know that feeling good about myself is just as important as looking good to others. I want my daughters to feel the same way.

—MO

Michelle's Undeniable Transformation

While Barack was being added to a short list for the Democratic nomination for president of the United States, Michelle was just settling into a new home with their two girls. But a new reality was quickly dawning.

"It was a lot to handle for her. I remember she and Barack coming out to Los Angeles for a series of formal events around that time and having to lend her evening bags because she had forgotten to pack them. Her life was moving incredibly fast and she didn't have time to catch her breath," recalls Mattie Lawson, a longtime friend of the Obamas.

Michelle didn't veer far from her predictable fashion favorites when she spent evenings out charming Obama supporters for votes. Her signature corporate wardrobe of skirts and pantsuits with tailored blazers made the rounds through-out her no-nonsense "tell it like it is" exchanges with voters. Michelle saw no reason the clothes or the conversation that had gotten her this far would need to shift. Why not tell Obama supporters a little more about the real Barack, the good and bad? But like it or not, being in the public eye meant things would have to change in Michelle's persona and in her unwavering fashion sense.

Michelle Obama epitomizes twenty-first-century style. She is accessible, glamorous, and chic. I love her classic elegance, whether she's wearing an emerging designer, a mass brand, or haute couture. Mrs. Obama represents the best of American style and exemplifies a modern approach to "First Lady" dressing.
—Lubov Azria, creative director, BCBG Max Azria

Beginning Again

Over the years Michelle had seen her life change in ways that had been unimaginable, but becoming the country's first African-American First Lady wasn't a notion she'd ever remotely considered. What would be expected of her as she journeyed on this uncharted path? Would every word out of her mouth be second-guessed and every move she made overly analyzed by a media ready for any misstep? Did she have the right look? The Chicago native wouldn't have to wait very long to find out the answers to those probing questions. By the time Barack secured the 2008 Democratic nomination the world was madly in love with him, but with Michelle, not so much.

From all accounts, Michelle's career-minded outfits and hard-nosed, straight-to-the-point business sense hadn't exactly resonated with her husband's adoring masses of fans. The warm and nurturing woman who behind closed doors doted on her husband and two little girls was being overshadowed by a stuffy, overly conservative wardrobe that had simply worn out its welcome. Like any woman of reasonable intelligence, Michelle only needed to hear about the issue once. She'd never met a problem she couldn't solve. Not to mention that like any caring wife she wanted to be a plus and not a minus to her husband's dreams, aspirations, and goals. "I'm pretty sure you've never seen Michelle wear anything that looks close to a traditional suit since she's been in White House," says Robin Givhan. "She let all that go." If changing her entire public persona at a moment's notice would help give her husband the political edge he needed, she would do just that.

> Michelle did what most women have to do at some point in their lives. She had to learn how to mesh the woman she was at home with the one at work and the one who appeared in public. She had to master being those three parts of herself whenever the situation arose. We all have to do it, just not in full view of the world.
>
> —Judy Smith, former White House press aide and professional crisis manager

Within days of her husband's Democratic nomination win, Michelle's tart and all-too-real comments on Barack as a regular man with flaws became a distant memory. As effortless as it may have seemed, for Michelle, facilitating such a drastic change in image and style was no easy task. But Michelle understood the endgame and was playing to win a chance to impact history. She wouldn't do it alone, either.

As quickly as she could she amassed a team of top stylists and makeup artists to help redefine the woman America needed to know better. The dark pin-striped suits and other stuffy gray attire were seamlessly replaced by colorful shift dresses like the ones once favored by Jackie Kennedy and lovely floral ensembles by designers like Tracy Reese and Rachel Roy, meant to convey the kind and loving tendencies Michelle Robinson Obama would and could display in the White House. If the dramatic change of direction in clothes and tone ever gave Michelle pause, she certainly never showed it. She waltzed very easily and without hesitation or reservation into a new and more acceptable version of herself for mainstream America and the world to embrace. And by doing so, she dutifully relinquished the right to wear uptight clothes that lacked warmth and personality. It's important to note that she didn't actually change who she was, only rearranged certain areas of her outward appearance to make peace.

There is so much for anyone to admire about the First Lady Michelle Obama. Her fashion sense, her career, her brilliant mind, and her wonderful marriage and her beautiful children. I love all of that about her and every time I see her, and any time I speak with her, I try to pick up a few tips for myself.

—Beyoncé

Purge Your Wardrobe and Prepare to Rebuild

It can be all too easy to fall into the same rut Michelle was in before diversifying her wardrobe. One way to avoid the boredom of sameness in your wardrobe is by doing a six-month purge of your closet. Doing this allows you to see what you have, what you don't have and what you have way too much of. This habit can actually save you money as it keeps you from repurchasing items that are too similar. Paring down and throwing out or donating clothes that no longer fit or aren't in style can also save you time by giving you a clear view of what you have.

To make deciding what clothes to ditch easier, try parting with items you haven't worn in a year or more. Sell them on eBay if they're still in pretty good shape. Or in the spirit of Michelle, find a local charity or women's shelter that can readily put to use the items you no longer need. Organizations such as Dress for Success collect professional attire from donors to provide wardrobes for women transitioning from welfare back into the workforce. Find an affiliate in your area that does the same. After discarding the items you no longer wear, arrange your clothes by item and color. This should make your morning routine a whole lot easier.

Michelle's style is effortlessly classy and strong. She has fun with her wardrobe while still making appropriate choices for the occasion. Her bold style exemplifies the type of woman she is—smart, courageous, and confident.

—Tracy Reese, fashion designer

Shop Smart

Before the days of top designers creating outfits specifically for her, Michelle and her friends loved to frequent stores known for selling designer looks at half price for themselves and their growing toddlers. Top discount stores that cater to women struggling to look sophisticated and stylish on a budget are as common as nail salons in most major cities. Check your local newspaper or browse your favorite local fashion bloggers for the names and addresses of stores that carry brands you covet, and certainly check out these big-deal discount stores.

- T.J.Maxx and Marshalls—The granddaddies of discount chains, these two stores are laced with designers like Gucci, St. John, Valentino, and Costume National. Recently, T.J.Maxx opened a boutique within some of its stores called Runway at Maxx that features high-end pieces. The key to finding good deals at these shops is going early and going often. Bargain hunting can be hard work!
- Nordstrom Rack—An offshoot of the Nordstrom chain, this outlet store sells the parent store's clearance merchandise for pennies on the dollar. The store offers a massive shoe section that includes deep discounts on top designers in a variety of styles and sizes. Nordstrom Rack also carries a fabulous selection of leather handbags and brand-name perfumes and lotions.

- Loehmann's—Another top discount store that houses the highest-quality designer clothes you can find at seriously reduced prices. Their yearly Italian sale is a joy to behold. Befriend a sales-clerk for clarification on days of designer deliveries. On the West Coast it's Wednesday mornings and in southern regions, deliveries usually occur on Tuesdays.

- J.Crew, Talbots, Banana Republic, and other less expensive alternatives that offer regular sales— Though not considered traditional discount stores per se, these reasonably priced shops that can be easily found in malls all over the country and offer wonderful pieces that can be mixed and matched for work, play, or evening wear. While on the campaign trail in early 2008, the fashion community couldn't stop talking about the airy blue-and-white windowpane sundress Michelle wore from the Gap with her beloved white cardigan tied around her shoulders. On her visit to the female-friendly talk show *The View* in 2008, Michelle wore a sleek high-waisted leaf-print dress from the store White House Black Market by designer Donna Ricco. As you continue to develop your wardrobe keep your eyes open for stores that offer great style for reasonable prices. Channel your inner Michelle and check the store's Web site for customers' comments on the longevity and durability of the clothes as well. A deal on anything isn't worth much if it falls apart shortly after purchasing.

Go the Extra Mile:
If you live in a major city try driving out to a store positioned closer to the outskirts of town. There a pair of Giuseppe Zanotti shoes for $199 may seem unreasonable to the locals and therefore will likely remain on the shelves in your size for weeks. They'll also be marked down within two to three weeks, allowing you to buy a pair of five-hundred-dollar shoes for less than one hundred dollars. Good times!

Michelle Obama has so many qualities that I like and admire for myself and I think a lot of the women that I design for have those same qualities or aspire to have those same qualities in their lives and personalities. She is in a sense my perfect client, the woman I think about when designing my clothes for every woman.

—Rachel Roy, fashion designer

The Known and the Unknown

In her twenties and thirties Michelle enjoyed shopping for classy designer outfits at bargain and discount stores with her girlfriends. As her fashion instincts grew, she developed an interest in wearing the creations of lesser-known designers such as Jason Wu and Maria Pinto—not exactly household names in the world of fashion and certainly not names associated with the likes of former First Ladies Jackie Kennedy and Nancy Reagan. In true Michelle style, the gutsy girl from Chicago had a plan for a new set of fashion rules she'd implement in the White House while her husband was in office. These new rules would allow her to deviate from the norm and test the limits of modern style in ways that would greatly benefit up-and-coming designers. Her new direction and thought on style would also mesh seamlessly with her husband's call for hope and change among a new generation of voters.

"Whereas Hillary Clinton and Laura Bush entered the White House still wearing the designs of people from their old world, Michelle immediately developed a relationship with Seventh Avenue by choosing Jason Wu to design her inauguration dress," says Robin Givhan. "She also had her own tried-and-true designers, but she sent a strong message to the fashion world by wearing Jason Wu and supporting a young, independent brand early on."

As her life in the White House unfolded, Michelle knew she could never underestimate the power of a flawless look while she stood next to the leader of the free world. Nor could she risk being chastised as a First Lady unaware of—or worse, unconcerned with—the dismal financial realities of the people and world around her. Former First Lady Nancy Reagan endured her share of stinging criticism during the eighties with her penchant for wearing expensive gowns from Bob Mackie and Adolfo while the country struggled with inflation. Unlike Jackie Onassis, who continues to be hailed for her timeless, classic style and savvy choice of designs, Nancy Reagan's years in the White House and her impact on fashion as a whole have been largely referenced as too over-the-top or too Hollywood for modern taste.

Change the Game

Michelle completely changed the fashion game with her fearless departure from the traditional and expected Washington uniform. She searched and found an acceptable path toward style success by mixing high-end designers with lower-priced designs from Target, the Gap, and H&M, which is something every woman can do. Not surprisingly Michelle's bold decision to support names not so familiar in the fashion world didn't exactly sit well with some of the industry gatekeepers once she moved into 1600 Pennsylvania Avenue. Of course that mattered very little to Michelle as she continued to stock her closet with American labels like Thakoon and Rachel Roy.

Embrace Your Mistakes

While Michelle's fashion instincts for the most part proved successful and universally applauded, she has made her share of style missteps, and rest assured you will too on your journey to fashion nirvana. One major and quite notable early fashion error was Michelle's decision to wear a rather fitted pair of khaki shorts during the family's 2009 vacation to Grand Canyon. Videos and pictures of the toned and shapely First Lady descending the steps of Air Force One caused quite a stir in both the news and fashion worlds. Many complained she was showing too much skin for a woman in her position, while others maintained the forty-plus-year-old mother of two looked fine.

The "Shortsgate" controversy was a huge wake-up call

for Michelle as she continued to struggle with meshing the private and public sections of her new world. Friends say that shortly before Michelle departed from the plane that day, she asked her staff if she should change into long pants. No one thought she should since she was on vacation. Wrong. When in doubt, follow your mind and your own gut instincts. Michelle clearly had reservations about the shorts and could have saved herself a world of trouble and bad headlines if she'd trusted her own misgivings. She's rarely been seen wearing a pair since. Just like Michelle, when you step outside your door, be it the White House or your house on Anywhere Avenue, remember you are representing you, and only you will face the consequences of whatever you decide to wear or not wear.

New Girls on the Block

From all accounts Michelle is as loyal to her favorite designers as she is to many of her girlfriends. She so adored her Azzedine Alaïa sleeveless knit dress that featured a ruffled skirt and tulle underlay that she bought the dress in four different colors. Perhaps the dress had special meaning because of its association with her earliest days as First Lady. She wore the first edition of the dress in black in 2009 while accompanying her husband to a NATO summit dinner in Baden-Baden, Germany. She paired it with a black knit bolero jacket and accessorized the ensemble with black heels, diamond hoop earrings, and a crystal cuff.

French president Nicolas Sarkozy and his wife Carla Bruni-Sarkozy were also in attendance at the dinner. In the days before the summit the media created much anticipation for the two First Ladies' initial introduction to one another.

Bruni-Sarkozy, a former model and singer, was expected to surely surpass Michelle Obama in the style and glamour department given her relative youth (she's four years younger than Michelle) and equally striking height of five foot nine. Bruni-Sarkozy indeed wowed in her wonderfully tailored Christian Dior outfits that weekend, but in the end, casual onlookers and fashion experts alike awarded the title of flawless and fabulous to Michelle. Her choice of Alaïa and of an eye-catching custom-made floral silk jacquard coat with a matching reverse-print dress underneath by the designer Thakoon clearly made her a darling of style on the international stage.

Mean Girls Need Not Apply

Michelle would face much stiffer competition on the effortlessly-flawless front in 2011 when she met Kate Middleton, the Duchess of Cambridge and wife of Prince William. Michelle and the president of the United States were formally introduced to the couple just a few weeks after the royal wedding in April of 2011. Kate wore a beige bandage dress by Reiss while Michelle shined in a pale green embroidered dress by Barbara Tfank and paired it with a cropped pink jacket, silver kitten heels, and a brooch. Though both women received top grades for their chic looks, the princess's simple form-fitting dress and loose flowing waves garnered the majority of the attention. Friends say Michelle rarely takes comparisons to other women for any reason to heart, preferring to embrace the sisterhood of friendship over the "I look better than she does" way of thought. Keep Michelle's view of life and relationships in mind when deciding what look works best for you. It's not a race to outdo the next woman in the room; it's about looking and feeling your best.

Women should feel confident in everything they wear while staying true to their personal style. Mrs. Obama knows her every move will be critiqued, but she still makes style choices which allow her to be comfortable in her own skin. It communicates a great level of poise and grace.

—Tracy Reese

Never End the Search

Take another tip from Michelle and discover your group of new designers by reading fashion and beauty blogs or by visiting local fashion shows in your area. While at Princeton Michelle took an interest in a few of her fellow classmates studying fashion design and supported them by modeling in their local fashion shows. Force yourself to step outside the norm by purchasing pieces you find at boutiques and smaller local stores that offer homegrown up-and-coming designers. In the early days of Obama's 2008 campaign, Michelle regularly supported the work of Chicago-based designers like Maria Pinto and Peter Soronen. Check out a few go-to fashion blogs along with some of Michelle's favorite fashion-forward minds in order to stay abreast of new faces on the style horizon.

Fashion Blogs to Keep You Fashion-Forward

The Zoe Report: The stylist known for creating looks for Nicole Richie, Anne Hathaway, and others, Rachel Zoe now has her own line of clothing, reality show, and Web site. Her fashion blog regularly reports about fashion, beauty, and lifestyle must-haves and you can sign up for daily e-mails with tips on current fashion news. Zoe also suggests alternatives to pricey runway fashions and young designers with similar styles to covet. (www.thezoereport.com)

StyleCaster: This fashion blog takes fashion-savvy women on trips to the actual showrooms of known and unknown designers while sharing tips on how to mix and match styles for different seasons and events. (www.stylecaster.com)

FabSugar: This site is a smorgasbord of fashion, beauty, tech, and more. The fashion section gives great tips and ideas on style and showcases various designers' spring and summer runway shows frame by frame. (www.fabsugar.com)

The Cut: A division of *New York* magazine, this Web site and blog gives great info on all things fashion, including tidbits on the world of modeling, designer secrets, and the latest info on celebrity fashion hits and misses. (nymag.com/daily/fashion)

Stylelist: This site offers videos with step-by-step ideas on how to put your wardrobe together for work and play, and includes interviews with designers where they dispense their own personal tips for looking good. (www.stylelist.com)

Michelle's A-List of Designers

Michelle quickly developed a love for a few favorite designers who offered collections that effortlessly blended expert craftsmanship with clean lines and creative embellishments. Since entering the White House in 2009, Michelle has proudly supported a long list of American designers while also embracing a few European and Japanese names as well. Below is a list of the designers Michelle leans toward when duty calls.

Isabel Toledo

This Cuban-born designer created the lemongrass wool lace dress lined with white silk that the First Lady wore on inauguration day. She also designs a line of budget-friendly shoes and accessories for Payless.

Jason Wu

Before Michelle Obama put this Taipei-born designer on the map by wearing his ivory chiffon, one-shoulder gown to the Inaugural Ball, he attended design school at Parsons in New York and was a finalist for the 2008 Vogue/CFDA Fashion Fund prize. He has also designed a line for Target to bring affordable designs to women across the country.

Maria Pinto

This Chicago native was responsible for the sheath dresses Michelle wore on the campaign trail, the most famous being the purple dress Michelle wore when she fist-bumped her husband during the campaign. She is now the creative director for Mark Shale's women's line, based in Chicago.

Tracy Reese

This African-American designer made the First Lady's floral dress for a *People* cover shortly after the Obamas entered the White House. Her collections sell at Nordstrom and she also designs a line of nail polish for Sally Hansen.

Peter Soronen

A Michigan native, his clothes focus on structure, reflected in his signature addition of corsets in most of his pieces. Soronen designed several outfits for Michelle while she was on the campaign trail and in the White House. Michelle reportedly loves Soronen's emphasis on small waists, which she luckily has.

Narciso Rodriguez

An American designer of Cuban descent, Rodriguez's family wanted him to become a dentist or a doctor. Instead he chose fashion and went on to work for the fashion houses of Anne Klein and Calvin Klein before launching his own label. He gained national attention in 1996 after designing Carolyn Bessette's wedding dress for her marriage to John F. Kennedy Jr.

He [Barack] is always asking, "Is that new? I've never seen that before." It's like, why don't you mind your own business? Solve world hunger. Get out of my closet.

—MO

A Girl and Her Fashion

While Michelle's striking profile and slim figure allow her to look amazing in couture clothing by the likes of Michael Kors and Naeem Khan, she looks equally fabulous in outfits pulled from stores like the Gap and Target. Her integration of these low-end and high-end pieces at any number of major political events is so seamless that onlookers would have a hard time distinguishing which ones came with the high price tags. Michelle makes no bones about letting her schedule for the day dictate her choice of clothes. For a 2011 interview at the White House the First Lady wore a pink sleeveless dress with a black bow from Target. She admitted to reporters at a White House round-table discussion on health and family that even the weather plays a crucial role in her fashion decisions: "My day-to-day wardrobe choices are very practical. I'm like, what's the temperature? Am I going to be sitting on the grass? Will I be playing with kids? I usually want to."

The Sum Total of All

Michelle's defining rule is to wear whatever style you choose and can afford with a confidence and pride that tells the world exactly who you are. Mixing and matching designer and budget duds is a skill, one that Michelle practices well. To determine what to spend and splurge on, use the quite helpful cost-per-wear measurement. You can find out the cost per wear by dividing the cost of the fashion item—be it clothing, shoes, a handbag, or an accessory—by how many times you plan to wear or use it. Save money in the long run by investing in quality classic pieces like these.

A good bag. You don't have to spend your month's rent on a Gucci bag or a Chloe tote, but you should purchase a purse that is made of sturdy leather and has a structured shape with reinforced stitching. Michelle has always shied away from items that display flashy labels that scream "designer," so follow her lead and stay away from logos and trendy colors and shapes, particularly if you want to use the handbag for years to come. Ever practical with her money, Michelle never saw the point in buying cheap knockoffs of designer goods. If you want that beautiful Marc Jacobs purse, save a few extra dollars each month until you have enough to own the actual item and enjoy.

A great dress. A great dress is one that you can take from your office to the party without giving it a second thought. It has a great shape that fits your body perfectly and makes heads turn when you walk into the room. Michelle owns quite a few of these and transitions from day to evening by adding a colorful shawl, diamond earrings, or a pearl necklace to create a more polished look. Remember, if two or more people compliment it every time you wear it, it's worth the price you paid.

A good bra. This is a lesson Michelle surely learned years ago but a surprisingly large number of women haven't. Remember that you're only as good as your foundation, and that begins with the items you wear *under* the fabulous clothes you invest in. Bras offer needed support that can help you maintain a youthful shape for years to come. Try upscale discount stores for good deals on undergarments that will last.

A great pair of shoes. Whatever style you prefer, pumps, sandals, clogs, or stylish flip-flops, make sure they're made of

quality leather and give your ankles, arch, and heels the cush-
ion they need to keep your feet free from ailments that can
cause you pain later. Michelle's shoe size and height made it
imperative she wear shoes that were well crafted. Treat your
feet with the same kindness.

Chapter Six
All the Single Ladies

I have freed myself to put me on the priority list and say yes, I can make choices that make me happy.

—MO

*H*ad Michelle known the adoring glances her future husband would be sending her way ten years after they first met, maybe she would have sought love out sooner. But according to those who know her well, Michelle was never in a rush to find love. As a young woman she didn't believe her existence was solidified or defined by her relationship status. Her older brother, Craig, insists that Michelle's thin dating résumé was mostly the result of her strong and unwavering ideas on what qualities the man in her life needed to have. Other good friends note the more obvious reason for Michelle's short dating list was the fact that Princeton and Harvard weren't exactly dating meccas for women of color in the eighties, leaving Michelle very few options for suitors.

Whatever the reason, most agree that Michelle simply had little desire to engage in the normal cat-and-mouse games many women and men play with one another when just starting out. Her own time was of the essence and better spent focusing on her future career and the needs of others. In her mind, any man she would become involved with would need to feel the same way. Ultimately the future First Lady chose not to spend her youth pondering her chances for a storybook romance. The man of her dreams would come along when the time was right. During her school years, Michelle turned the majority of her attention to her studies, personal development, and community activism. She knew that she'd have to become the "who" she eventually wanted to attract.

Take a hint from Michelle's way of thinking and use the time you have between romances or before meeting "the one" to get to know who you are and what you bring to and desire from a relationship. If you are single, use this time to improve upon any aspect of yourself and your life that you feel needs it. Michelle kept active and upbeat as she began to build a satisfying life that would eventually include a man to share it with. Follow her lead in this chapter by learning the importance of being true to your ideals and preferences while developing a solid plan to find the soul mate you desire.

The Fine Art of Being Alone

Take a moment to enjoy the wonderful feeling of solitude and the freedom being alone allows. Before marrying Barack, Michelle made the most of being a young single woman. She finished law school, hung out with friends, traveled around the country, attended concerts and movies, and did quite frankly whatever she wanted to do with her own time. Being in a relationship where you share the highs, lows, ups, and downs of life can be a beautiful thing, but having the chance to spend some quality time with yourself is something to relish. The best part? Once your soul mate makes an entrance, you'll be mentally relaxed, emotionally refreshed, and physically ready to welcome him with open arms. Michelle would wholeheartedly approve of this approach. Be sure to appreciate the following:

"Me" time. Do you just love curling up with a good book, mud mask on your face, and trusty leopard-print head scarf wrapped around your hair on the weekends? Of course you do. Understand that those days will be few and far between when a new love comes around. So enjoy them now, because your "me" time will soon become "we" time. Are you ready?

No checking in. For an adult woman, checking in to let others know where you are at all times has long become a thing of the past. That could change when someone new comes along. When you're in a relationship, the other person cares and wants to know where you are and if you're okay. Enjoy the luxury of only answering to yourself while you can.

Lonely for the right reasons. Being lonely while single is far better than feeling alone in a relationship, and yes, that happens to many couples. Being taken for granted or being neglected by a partner is about as lonely as it gets. So appreciate that the loneliness you may feel right now is self-imposed and can end at any time.

Meeting new people. Dating can be a frustrating experience, but admit it—meeting new people is pretty exciting.

When you're in a committed relationship, you're with just one person and that can be a beautiful thing. But while you're single, enjoy the opportunity to meet and greet new men and just have fun.

No need to compromise. You want Chinese. He wants seafood. You prefer dialogue-driven love stories, he prefers the latest explosion-filled action film—that's what happens in a relationship. Couples have to compromise and there's no successful way around it. Enjoy the chance to be a little selfish in your choices of movies and takeout while you can.

What to Do in the Meantime

As you continue to seek the partner, lover, and/or relationship you've dreamed of having for years, continue to clear and clean out your closet, both physically and mentally. Finding love will require doing a little work on your own issues if you want to attract the right someone. Take this time to develop, create, and fulfill some of the lifelong passions that have been hanging around in the back of your mind. Be they big or small, this is the time to just go for it. Throw caution to the wind and enroll in that screenwriting class you've always wanted to try or learn how to play a killer game of chess with the ladies at church. Expanding your own world will only enhance the interest of those you meet. Adding new hobbies to your life can also aid in the elimination process, a process that may unfortunately need to be repeated again and again throughout your lifetime. Getting rid of the clutter in your life can mean reaching back to the past to address painful childhood woes or releasing the hurt of a more recent relationship that left you rather bitter. Those issues won't mesh with a new love any better than unresolved daddy issues will. Whether you're young and never had a serious relationship, in the middle of a nasty breakup, or ready to get back on the horse again after a failed romance, take some time to work on you. If you don't, you run the very real risk of making the same mistakes twice, resulting in the same disappointment and heartbreak.

Break the cycle and learn from past experiences. If there is any one remarkable quality to absorb from Michelle, it's her uncanny ability to be completely truthful with herself. If something needed to be changed about her actions and attitude, she was open to doing just that. So go ahead and ask yourself the hard questions. Do you regularly find yourself attracted to men who are emotionally unavailable, or worse, emotionally stunted? Have a number of your dates already had a significant other or been overly involved in their work? Do you bend over backward in a relationship, attempting to please the other person, even if it means sacrificing your own pleasure and happiness?

A good deal of these traits and behaviors can be associated with any number of emotional traumas and issues, but studies have also shown repeatedly that several of these debilitating characteristics are exhibited regularly by women who grow up without the attention and love of a beloved father. So woman up, look in the mirror and decide if any of these apply to you. Ask a valued friend for an honest evaluation of your "type" and/or how you behave in a relationship. Then act accordingly. There's no need to live a perpetual Groundhog Day. Taking the time to think about how your past affects your present isn't easy, but it is necessary if you plan on being and feeling worthy of healthy love.

Daddy's Girl

In life and love, Michelle benefited immensely from the most vital measuring stick any woman needs in her search for true love and companionship. She came of age in a home with a mother and father who clearly loved one another and worked together to form a strong partnership that included doing what was best for their two children. Witnessing day in and out exactly how a man should treat a woman—with respect and value—and how a woman should do the same afforded Michelle a solid foundation for developing and defining her own healthy relationship with the man of her dreams. Her father, Fraser, had served as a living and breathing example of how a "good man" lived, acted, reacted, and treated those he loved most. Studies indicate that girls who grow up with their fathers fully present and in the home are more likely to get better grades, attend college, and have healthy relationships. Michelle got the long end of the stick.

It wasn't very easy to pass muster with my sister, particularly for the men she would date. They had a tough test to pass with her.

—Craig Robinson

Rule of Thumb No. 13: Consider Your Compatibility

Michelle determined early on that anyone seeking to share a moment of all she had to offer would have to be worthy. That attitude didn't exactly aid in expanding her dating prospects. But while she didn't hit the town every weekend back in the day, when she did, Michelle made a point of dating men she felt compatible with, men she'd noticed before due to either a fascinating conversation she'd had with them or their shared mutual interests. She knew judging a person by anything else would ultimately lead to a boring and disappointing dead end. Follow Michelle's lead all the way on this one. Choosing a potential partner based only on physical attraction isn't enough. Michelle figured out early on that looks do fade, cars do get repossessed, and clothes do come in and out of style. Base your attraction and interest on something more tangible if you are looking for sincere love for the long haul.

On occasions when she did spend time with a gentleman, Michelle routinely compiled mental notes of all the things she liked and admired about her date as well as the traits and attributes she just couldn't abide. Sound a bit much? Not for the future Mrs. Obama. In Michelle's very organized world of thought, the best way to find true love was similar to the very best way to find a great job: Identify what you want in and from a relationship and stay true to those ideals throughout. Of course, like Michelle, do remember to be a little flexible in matters of the heart. Leaving a little wiggle room for the unknown in life and for love to occur is always highly recommended.

In the end Michelle understood well what you must learn. Only *you* know what makes you happy, content, and satisfied in a relationship. And if you don't know, take this time to find out. You are also the only keeper of your real relationship hang-ups. You, not your roommate or your well-intentioned mother, can guide yourself in the right direction. Therefore it's your responsibility to pinpoint what makes you happy and how best to find it. Michelle was never confused about this truism.

Get in the Game

Once you feel confident that you've truly been introspective about your past and present, you can begin to ever-so-slowly dabble in the world of dating. In the good ole days, around the time Michelle met Barack, people connected with one another the old-fashioned way: through friends of friends, in class, at work, or simply by saying hello to someone who caught their eye. Unfortunately today it seems a great deal more work has to be done before finding your perfect match, and it usually involves something as initially impersonal as sitting on your couch with your computer in hand. Studies show one in five relationships begins online, so don't dismiss this vital tool for meeting your soul mate.

If you're new to online dating it can be a bit daunting at first, not to mention costly. Start with the trial versions of one or two of the more well-known and well-regarded dating organizations, such as Match.com or eHarmony.com. Both go to great lengths to pinpoint your interests, wants, and needs and then to pair with you someone complementary. A trial will allow you a chance to become familiar with the process and check out the candidates you'll have to choose from without the commitment. If you're interested in more self-examination, complete the in-depth questionnaire on Chemistry.com and let that system take a scientific approach to matching you with a mate. If your first priority is to meet someone with similar interests, try HowAboutWe.com, a site that lists date ideas to choose from, rather than profiles, and connects people based on the ideas they like. The beauty of online dating is the chance to meet people you probably would never have the chance to in real life. You can meet people completely out of your inner circle inside the comfort of your home. Fire-fighters, software designers, and rocket scientists are in search of love too, so remember to keep an open mind while enjoying the process.

Virtues and Vices

There's no doubt that Michelle had great examples and a crystal-clear vision of the man she desired to spend her life with. Her requirements in and from a mate were based on the deeply rooted beliefs and values she'd embraced her entire life. The traits Michelle saw in her parents' marriage were the requirements she held most near and dear in her search for true love. She rarely veered from her desire to find a man who was honest, respectful, and caring in the ways that mattered in the long run. A man who valued family and loyalty in much the same way her father had was tops on Michelle's list.

Once you decide to seriously conquer the dating world, be sure you're able to distinguish a quality you like and need from a petty quirk that means very little in the long run. Review your list of requirements in a mate and ask yourself why they mean so much to you and if they are fair. On a more serious note, Michelle hated the fact that Barack smoked when they met and worked endlessly to break him of that bad habit. It took quite a few years of hard-core persuading, but she did eventually help him say good-bye to that unhealthy vice.

In your search for a new love, don't lose out on something or someone potentially amazing because you're hung up on some unreasonably silly deal breaker, like these.

Height. Most women say they prefer their men to be three to four inches taller than they are. Consider for a moment what would have happened if Michelle, at five eleven, had the same criteria regarding height: Where would she be? Not in the White House. Word to the wise—only 10 percent of the population is over six feet, so either ditch the stilettos or get over it.

Level of success. What constitutes success usually varies from person to person. But if you're a highly paid executive with her own home and a master's degree, a guy at the entry level or who isn't as educated might not be the best match for you. On the other hand, remain reasonable and don't look down on someone who is on the right track but not quite far enough along to reap the rewards—yet.

Living condition. While a man still living under his parents' roof can be a bit off-putting at first, do a little research before you totally rule him out. Is he there to care for his ill or elderly parents or did he hit financial hardship in his job and needed a place to start over? Life can be harsh sometimes, so give people slack when warranted.

Rule of Thumb No. 14: Date for Potential

Michelle offered no apologies for her no-nonsense approach to life or the lofty desires and dreams she had for herself. She loved a good time out on the town like everyone else (she enjoyed hanging with her girls during happy hour on Fridays in Cambridge) but saw little need to spend it with someone who didn't bring stimulating conversation or add something else of note to her life. It didn't have to be an engagement ring or a small island in Fiji, but it certainly had to be something she felt enhanced who she already was. After all, she had a wide range of gifts to offer anyone who decided to spend time with her. So, if you've already met a new guy and you're hitting it off pretty well, ask yourself if he's the one for the long haul or if he's only the one for right now. Or is this just a friendship with benefits? It's important for you to understand and appreciate what you're doing and why you're doing it. If you're a person who just loves a good time with no strings attached, by all means go ahead and have one. But make sure both parties involved understand where it is or isn't headed. Men may sometimes enter relationships without thinking it through, but, woman, you're better served by always having your wits about you in love, life, and play.

Boy Meets Girl

Life can lead you down some pretty winding roads and some of those roads may bypass one another at first, before eventually reconnecting in the end. Michelle Robinson graduated from Harvard Law School in May of 1988, while her future husband enrolled at Harvard in September of that very same year. Though Barack was a few years older than Michelle, he'd opted to take a few years off from school before applying to law school, preventing the two from meeting on the lush Ivy League campus. But as the wonderful hand of fate would have it, their paths would cross just a year later, back in Michelle's hometown of Chicago.

After just one year of employment, Michelle had already impressed the powers that be at Sidley Austin, the prestigious law firm where she landed a job after graduating from Harvard. In fact, her bosses were so thrilled with her work that they asked her to mentor a few incoming summer interns. The interns would get a taste of legal life under the

tutelage of established lawyers during the day and the opportunity to socialize with the newer members of the law
firm in the evenings. One of the interns Michelle would have
charge of for the summer just so happened to be a super-cute
guy with a very unique name—Barack Obama.

Michelle loves to recount the times her coworkers mentioned what a perfect date the cute new intern would be for
her. He was smart and over six feet. Perfect for Michelle's
five-eleven stature. And to have been chosen as an intern after completing just one year of law school at Harvard, he had
to be incredibly bright. Barack Obama was special, and of
course he was also black, a fact that wasn't lost on Michelle
when coworkers attempted to link them together. She found
the assumption that the only two African-Americans at the
company should become romantically involved particularly
amusing.

She was possibly the most ambitious associate that I've ever seen.
—Quincy White, retired senior partner at Sidley Austin

Michelle greeted Barack on his first day, still amused by
the suggestion, and invited him to a work lunch in order to
make him feel at home and to discuss all aspects of the internship. Surprisingly, she instantly found his conversation smart,
witty, and gap-free. She also decided he was far cuter than the
pictures he'd sent in with his application. The two talked the
entire meal without the slightest break in dialogue or hint of
pretension. Michelle was impressed by their connection, to
say the least, but could also sense Barack's personal interest.
That was a concern for her. As a woman, the only African-

American at the firm no less, Michelle felt the strong need to walk a straight line at her place of employment. She'd worked hard to get to where she was and she wasn't about to let any office romance ruin it.

Immediately I liked him because he didn't take himself seriously, but he was very bright, had an interesting background, just a good guy to talk to.

—MO

Love on the Job

If you're considering an office liaison, heed Michelle's warning and give it the necessary thought it requires by considering these three questions:

- Are you up-and-coming in your job, still trying to gain traction with the higher-ups? If so, tread slowly and quietly.
- How have other office trysts fared in the end? These types of connections happen all the time (after all, we spend most of our waking hours in the company of our coworkers), but the particulars of similar past circumstances are a necessary point of reference.
- Can the two of you handle a budding romance discreetly? Follow your gut reaction and honor your inner feelings. If you have a nagging vibe that it's not such a good idea to hook up at the office, then by all means stay unhooked.

Pique His Interest

From all accounts, Barack was completely dazzled by Michelle from their very first exchange. Friends say the future president of the United States often recalls being mesmerized by the Chicago native's charm, beauty, and intellect at first glance. Always make an effort to look and be at your best, but don't forget to keep him intrigued—these are the tips that will take you to that desired first date and beyond.

Smile. This is the most important addition to any wardrobe, so don't leave home without it. When the man you'd love to impress or the one you didn't even realize had you in his sights sees you smile, he sees a woman who is happy and exuding positive energy. What could be more attractive than that?

Pay him a compliment. When you compliment a man, he feels really good about himself. There isn't a deed that compares to lifting another's spirits. When you make the man you'd like to get to know better feel good, he'll attribute his upbeat mood to you and automatically want to see you more. Quick, easy, and effective.

Mind your words in the beginning. It's in our nature as women to share our thoughts and feelings. But in this case, whoever says the least holds the power. During Michelle's first lunch with Barack, she allowed him to discuss his background and ideals for the future for the majority of the conversation, holding much about who she was close to the vest. Letting the man do most of the talking during the infancy of a relationship makes him comfortable, while you get the jump on any personality issues.

Maintain eye contact. Look him, and anyone you meet, in the eye at least 30 percent of the time when you speak to them. It's a sign of confidence on your part and it's how men relate in the business world. It's also Body Language 101. Eye-to-eye contact creates trust and puts people at ease.

Have some fun. Life is serious enough. Lighten up and show the guy who's caught your eye how funny your funny bone is. A man wants to know that the woman he's interested in can let loose and have fun. Tease him in an affectionate way or tell him a non-graphic off-color joke. Do anything that takes the pressure off of getting to know each other.

Stay classy. Behaving as a lady may seem like something from a Jane Austen novel, but the overall impact of remaining poised and feminine can never be underestimated. If you feel or have been told you fall short in this category, check out YvonneandYvettetiquette.com, a Web site run by two sisters who share their etiquette advice for the twenty-first century. They also hold "Modern Manners" workshops if you think you might need a more intensive how-to.

Cute's good, but cute only lasts for so long, and then it's, who are you as a person?

—MO

A Few Things You Should Know by the End of the First Date

Michelle and Barack went to a Spike Lee movie on their real first date, and a stroll through Chicago's Art Institute followed soon after. Michelle was clearly smitten with the man who didn't seem to mind being openly romantic and attentive to her needs. In Barack, she felt she'd finally met someone on the same page in life with the same ideals and with a mind open to exploring places like fabulous art collections and hidden jewels of the city. Thankfully, Barack was in many ways an open book when he met Michelle, relatively in touch with his own feelings and emotions and not afraid to share them. Many men aren't and won't be so forthcoming. Being wined and dined is indeed marvelous, but don't let the experience of someone simply treating you nicely blind you. Get to know him. Reach out and get beneath the layers of what you see and find out who he is beyond that great smile.

What are his interests and hobbies? Is he a car fanatic or hiking fiend? Does he check ESPN's *SportsCenter* site on his phone several times a day? Does he even have time to spare for these types of things? All these questions are the hallmark of good solid conversation and they give the relationship a chance to grow.

Where does he work? Michelle had the luxury of meeting her new man at work, but depending on how your paths cross, you may need to ask questions to establish whether he's employed and if so, where. No need for salary info or his place in line for the next promotion at the office. Just the basics will do for now.

Does he have kids? In this day and time meeting a man without children is about as easy as finding Louis Vuitton on sale. Blended families are quite the norm but that doesn't mean you shouldn't get a few things clarified before heading in.

Now that you're well aware of the vital questions to ask on a first date, it's important to note the subjects you need not broach as well. Topping that list: your last relationship, your family's mental health, any bankruptcy filings, and your number of sexual partners. All nice men aren't good men, so sharing your personal info with someone you just met is bad business.

Rule of Thumb No. 15: Play It Cool

Some women are rather quick to assume, if not declare, that they've met Prince Charming after only a few moments in his presence. This was clearly not a problem Michelle struggled with during her dating days. She took her time assessing the men she met carefully and rarely fell head over heels after a first date. Neither should you. Why the rush anyway? Oftentimes, being alone doesn't sit well in a society that constantly sells us on the idea that everyone must be paired off, for better or worse. Rushing into a relationship, no matter the reason, is a surefire way of ending up lost, confused, and heartbroken. More than likely, you've already been down that road. So, why return?

If you need more evidence that rushing love is a bad idea, consider this—as a rule men say they often date with no real expectations, allowing them to actually have fun while getting to the know the other person. So, why would you begin designing wedding invitations or choosing dinner-table settings after just the second date? No matter if you're twenty, thirty, or even forty years old and beyond, it's never too late to have fun and learn a new thing or two while playing the dating game.

Beyond the First Date

While you're playing the dating game, choose activities that help you get to know each other better. Men love action, and studies show they open up more and engage in conversation freely while involved in activities that require constant motion. Keep that in mind when planning afternoon or evening outings with your beau. Try at least one of these romantic escapades to promote real intimacy in your budding relationship.

Bicycle rides in the park. A nice bike ride through the park or along the beach gets the romance flowing through a good old-fashioned time for the two of you, not to mention the health benefits you'll be receiving from the workout and the natural glow you'll have after it's over.

Bowling. This sport has been around since your parents'— or possibly your grandparents'—dating days, and there's a reason it remains a popular night out on the town. Michelle and Barack are said to have enjoyed a few bowling-night double dates during their courtship and so should you. Bowling allows you to be competitive in a silly sort of way, while also allowing time to talk.

Book fairs and street festivals. A chance to roam around hand in hand while learning more about each other's interests and passions. Big cities such as Chicago, where Michelle and Barack began dating, usually have numerous such events each month. Check your local paper to see what your city has to offer.

Ice-cream run. As a teenager, Barack worked at Baskin-Robbins in Hawaii. In tribute to his past, he regularly took

Michelle to the local Baskin-Robbins for a scoop during the hot summer months in Chicago. You never know when or where you'll learn the most fascinating facts about your guy, so don't skip your scoop.

Dinner. Even today the Obamas make time for date night, often opting for a long dinner and sometimes dancing. Dining and romance create a tried-and-true evening to remember and never get old.

Confident vs. Clingy

Don't allow your excitement or anticipation about a new beau to throw you off your game. Your dignity and poise must remain intact even if the apple of your eye closely resembles Denzel Washington and may very well be the one. Though Michelle enjoyed her time with Barack on dates and over drinks, she was careful not to appear overanxious. She allowed him to suggest their early dates and followed his lead on the pace of the relationship in the early stages. She knew holding on too tightly to a man is never advisable. Give your relationship and yourself time to breathe while asking yourself: Are you confident or clingy?

> *Your potential new beau says he'll call at eight and he hasn't.*
> *Confident:* You send one e-mail asking if all is okay. How he handles this situation will speak volumes about his character and his place, or lack thereof, in your future.
> *Clingy:* You call his cell every five minutes and leave numerous messages until he responds or turns his

phone off. Also, you check his Twitter page to see if he's updated it.

You're enjoying a nice conversation with the adorable guy from your grad school class or church trustee board. You suggest the two of you meet for coffee sometime. He answers that his schedule is crazy most days so he'll have to check.
Confident: "No worries, I completely understand." "Too busy" usually means he's not interested, so take the hint. There will be other opportunities.
Clingy: You fire back that you could meet to go over an upcoming project to fit yourself into his schedule.

You meet a guy at a party and the interest seems mutual. He chats you up the entire evening and at the end of the night, you exchange numbers.
Confident: You wait a few days. You just met him, so give it some time. If he's eager to speak to you, he'll call. You can call too, but no need to rush it.
Clingy: You text him the same day to make sure he's remembered to save your pertinent info in his phone. You also ask if he has plans for the next few days.

If It Doesn't Work Out

In your quest to find true love you're bound to run into one or two men who seem absolutely perfect for you after only a few dates. You may hit it off immediately through a conversation, like Michelle and Barack, or instantly feel some physical connection, but over the course of a few more meetings you realize the two of you don't quite click as well as you should.

You may have discovered he isn't quite as polite or polished as you'd like or that he has the unfortunate habit of stiffing the waitstaff. Some personality traits and attributes are there for the long haul, so don't waste your time trying to change a man. As tempting as it may be to hold on to someone who seemed so close to being the one, do yourself a favor and realize that not all dates turn into full-fledged relationships. Some people come into your life to teach you lessons about who and what is right for you and who isn't. Take it all in and then move on.

Make the First Move

It isn't too far-fetched to imagine Michelle going after exactly what she wants in life and in love. So can you. The taboo of a woman asking a man out on a date disappeared years ago, freeing women to have much more control over the men they end up meeting. If someone special has caught your eye, summon your inner Michelle and approach him with complete confidence in what you have to offer. Always approach the object of your fascination by yourself. No girlfriends allowed for this venture. It could distract your intended target from the main attraction—you.

To avoid any awkward moments, play the conversation over in your head a few times before making your move. You want to come off cool and calm during your exchange. Whether you are at a party or a club, simply ask him what he's planning to order from the bar. While speaking to him, be as charming as you can without overdoing it. Too cute can be too much. If you just can't think of a conversation starter, play the fake familiarity game. Tell him he reminds you of someone and ask if he attended a certain college or high school. If he seems receptive, ask his name anyway. If he seems annoyed or uninterested, apologize and politely make your exit. You won't make a connection with everyone you meet. On to the next one.

Ready to Commit

When you have made a true connection with someone, you know. If you've met the man you feel is right and hope it's the real deal, make sure you are on the same page. It's difficult to imagine Michelle not having a straightforward conversation about the future with Barack the summer they met before he headed back to Harvard in the fall. Many women tiptoe around the very question they most desperately want answered, for fear of hearing the wrong response or, worse, running the man off. Michelle wasn't one to continue a relationship without some idea of where it was headed. Neither should you.

When the timing is right, have a frank discussion with your beau. Are you seeing other people? Are you guys having such a good time together that you're ready to settle down but he's still keeping his options open? You need to bite the bullet and find out.

Once that's settled, if marriage is an important next step for you, you probably want to find out whether this commitment means a walk down the aisle at some point in the future. Barack had a less-than-traditional view on marriage (more on this later), while Michelle valued the sanctity of marriage and sharing vows. Two people can have a committed relationship without marriage. Think Oprah and Stedman or Goldie and Kurt. You probably also know a few not-so-famous people with the same setup. This situation works for some and not for others. If you're similar to Michelle and want your partner to put a ring on it, make that clear. The art of determining where your man stands on the subject of marriage—and more importantly, marriage to you—can be a tricky feat. Use Michelle's truly brilliant way of getting to the heart of the matter by sharing a bit of your own thoughts on the subject early on (not too early—only you know when the time is right) and by really listening to what your prospective mate is saying. Michelle used her trademark straightforward approach with Barack but also backed up her no-nonsense stance with not-so-obvious hints regarding her wishes for a life that included marriage. At what she deemed appropriate moments, say just after a romantic film, Michelle would slyly reference the benefits marriage provided her parents over the years. At other times she'd recount to her then-boyfriend the many warm memories she had of a childhood anchored by two parents fully committed to one another. Occasions spent with friends who were either engaged or married also allowed the idea of marriage to take root in the back of Barack's mind.

Michelle's approach took savvy and tons of confidence, which of course Michelle had and still has. If you don't feel comfortable with a direct approach, do some background research. In the most subtle way you can find, enlist his friends, siblings, or parents in your quest to find out where his head may be on the marriage front. They may have valuable input on his attitude and on the future the two of you may have. Whatever method you use, be prepared to act if it's not the answer you like.

Chapter Seven
Love That Keeps Growing

I often tease Barack. He's incredibly smart, and he is very able to deal with a strong woman, which is one of the main reasons he can be president, because he can deal with me.

—MO

*D*eciding Barack was indeed the perfect man for her life and the future she envisioned was a very big deal for Michelle. After acknowledging and accepting Barack as her soul mate, Michelle began to transition into the next phase of her adult life: coupledom. Friends insist Michelle was convinced Barack was indeed the man of her dreams shortly after they met. She was drawn to his love of life, his incredible mind, and the fact that he seemed to take her ideas and dreams as seriously as he took his own. She could talk to Barack about anything and he'd listen intently while offering sensible advice on everything from her choice of jobs to her choice of friends. Michelle trusted her instincts and her instincts told her a life with

Barack was definitely in her future. With that in mind, she was determined to put in the work to make it happen. Of course, the future First Lady rarely did anything halfway in life. Though she and Barack would spend their first year or so together dating via phone, letters, and long-weekend visits while he finished law school in Boston, Michelle stayed true to her mantra that anything worth having was worth working for. So she dug her heels firmly in and embarked on the process of establishing a relationship built to last.

Michelle hated game playing and hated anyone who played games, particularly men. Barack wasn't that guy. He took life seriously and he took the people in his life seriously. Michelle bonded with that immediately. He was the man she'd hoped existed, come to life.

—Michelle's former coworker at Sidley

Professor Charles Ogletree believes his two former students at Harvard Law School were naturally connected by their intense desire for success and willingness to go above and beyond to reach it.

"They were a few months apart at Harvard and never met. Yet I feel they were destined to meet and connect at some point. It came as no surprise to me that they got together and developed the non-wavering bond they still share today. It was meant to be," he says.

Michelle clearly felt so, and those thoughts were only intensified by the relationship's continued growth even after the two were a thousand miles apart.

Nurturing a long-lasting relationship requires determination like Michelle's to establish a middle ground. The fact that her relationship was indeed a partnership was one of the first lessons Michelle took to heart, and it should be for you too. Your romantic future can't and won't be very bright if you don't abide by the give-and-take rules Michelle so seamlessly embraced from the moment she met her future husband. Because she'd seen all that a loving relationship entailed by watching her parents, Michelle was fully prepared to accept the ups and downs that came along with merging her life with a new mate's. From learning to bond with a future sister-in-law to adjusting to the unique and more time-consuming way he likes to wash clothes, relationships take patience, hard work, and sometimes, depending on your disposition, a keen sense of humor. Michelle relished the idea of forming a union with Barack that would be solid enough to weather any challenge they'd face. You can do the same by adopting a few of the more proactive techniques Michelle employed to help her relationship thrive.

Let a Man Be a Man

One of the major lessons Michelle learned early in life was the importance of letting a man be a man. She watched both her father and brother handle life and its varied circumstances in their own ways and with their own strength and fortitude. She understood that women and men have separate roles in relationships and all goes much smoother in love when both parties recognize that fact. Give the man in your life the room and opportunity to be who he really is. It begins with simple things like allowing him to pay for dinner and open the car door when you exit, actions that show courtesy as well as respect for you and your relationship. While some hard-core feminists may disagree with the theory that men were born to provide, Michelle understood that this prevailing thought process doesn't mean women aren't able to take care of themselves.

She also realized that men are born with the desire to pursue, so it's usually best to let a man express interest and make contact first, exactly the way Barack did. Allowing the man who asked you out to pay for dinner doesn't make you a gold digger, and waiting for him to make the first move doesn't suggest you're playing games. These rather easy and uncomplicated moves, when made early on, can form a foundation based on the security of knowing what roles each of you will accept further down the road. Each of you will have parts to play on the path to a successful relationship. The sooner you figure out what they are, the smoother your ride there will be.

Passing the Test

Once Michelle decided to take a chance on the fledgling young lawyer with the fascinatingly unique background, she faced the difficult prospect of maintaining a long-distance relationship. Early on she had an honest conversation with herself about the pros and cons and ultimately decided Barack was worth the large phone bill and the extra effort. Still, before Barack left town he'd have to pass another type of test— meeting Michelle's family and friends and suiting up for an important game of basketball with her older brother. It wouldn't be easy or typical. Michelle rarely brought her dates to the family's Chicago home for dinner. "Not that she dated a lot, because she didn't," her brother Craig explains. "It was hard to pass muster with my sister."

According to Craig, if a man made enough of an impression to inspire an invite to meet Michelle's family, he'd then have to pass a test that may seem a bit unusual and over-the-top to some. Apparently, Michelle's father believed strongly that a man's real character was shown on the basketball court—not in some stuffy boardroom. Heeding that advice, Michelle suggested Barack and Craig hit the courts to play ball. Though not a candidate for the NBA, Obama displayed pretty solid skills on the hardwood and apparently gave Craig, a top player in college, a good run for his money. The game spoke to Barack's basketball prowess but said even more about his willingness to go above and beyond for his new love. This wasn't lost on Michelle or her big brother.

"He wasn't a soft guy. He was aggressive without being a jerk and I was able to report back to my sister that this guy was first-rate," Craig recalls.

Even if you don't have access to an involved father or a concerned older brother to check out your new guy, make sure to invite him on outings with your friends and family once you've gotten to know him a bit. It doesn't have to mean a formal introduction; just watching him get along in a new situation with unfamiliar faces will go a long way in determining the boundaries of his comfort zone. It will also give those who know you best a chance to form and give an objective opinion of your new beau. Friends can be brutal and sometimes overly harsh on new recruits, but it stems from how much they care, and brutal honesty may be exactly what you need if this guy has taken measures to blind you to the real person he is inside. A serious crush or love-struck feelings can diminish your ability to distinguish good and bad or acceptable vs. unacceptable behavior. Your friends can help you get a more objective and well-rounded view of this new person in your life.

Rule of Thumb No. 16: Make It Last Forever

Michelle fully grasped the layered complexity of her new beau's background, along with its impact on him as a person and as a partner. On cozy dates for ice cream or walks after dinner and a movie, Barack would share with Michelle his rather unconventional experiences as a young interracial boy. Michelle took to heart his stories of his African-born father who'd left the family shortly after Barack was born. And she deeply felt her new love's pain when he explained he'd only met his father once before the elder Obama was killed in an automobile accident in his homeland.

Barack's story and journey were his own, so Michelle took great measures to appreciate those circumstances and the world he'd grown up in. As a true show of faith, she revealed those facts to very few people early on. Friends and family say it was months, if not longer, before they found out anything significant about the young man Michelle had become smitten with. Barack never mentioned his mother's or father's racial makeup or his rather nomadic childhood with his mother before he moved to Hawaii to live with his grandparents full-time. Michelle's brother, Craig, assumed the intricate details of the new boyfriend's younger days hardly mattered given that Barack probably wouldn't last long in his sister's life. Big brother was wrong, but what's more important to note here is Michelle's savvy intuition to follow Barack's lead regarding when and where to discuss his personal life. Her new gent, for reasons of his own, didn't feel comfortable discussing his splintered family with new acquaintances.

Michelle realized and respected his position by allowing him to tell his story to others when he felt ready to do so and not a minute before. A small gesture can mean a lot. Demonstrating that you're observant and considerate of your beau's feelings, emotions, likes, and dislikes is one of the first steps in gaining his trust and assuring he'll treat you the same way. During the early stages of a relationship, men may not always be as gregarious as you'd like, opting to avoid putting their insecurities and fears on full display. Women are usually far more observant and attentive to the little things in life. Why not use those qualities to show how much you care by honoring his feelings?

Meet Him Where He Is

Barack often referred to Michelle's storybook childhood and loving family life as something akin to *The Adventures of Ozzie and Harriet*. That was his exact reaction to meeting the Robinsons for the very first time in their Chicago home. The popular fifties television show featured the daily lives of a picture-perfect family seemingly always pleasant and loving to one another. Rather than being taken aback by her new beau's sugary-sweet reference, she instantly recognized his pointed observations about her family unit were really an even more pointed commentary on his own nontraditional childhood. "I think when he met Michelle and her family he saw the life he'd always wanted and now saw a way of becoming a part of the family he'd always silently yearned for," Patrick Riley, a student and friend of Barack's from the University of Chicago, explains. A traditional family with a father at the helm and a loving mother there to address all issues and needs was not a reality Barack experienced, and that impacted all aspects of his adult life. Given his complicated and somewhat nomadic background, Michelle knew a certain amount of patience and understanding would be necessary for their union to go the distance.

The partner of your dreams may very well arrive at your door with a set of oversize baggage at his side. Some people aren't worth the baggage fee, while others, like Barack, can be worth the extra charge if handled with care. In this day of broken families and single-parent households, your beloved beau may have any number of personal issues that caused him to stumble on the path to a healthy relationship. Borrow from Michelle's smarts by meeting your partner exactly where he is when it comes to nurturing and maintaining meaningful bonds. Try not to expect more than you know he is able to give as the relationship matures, and talk with each other regularly about your mutual wants, desires, and needs. These may change over time so keep the dialogue free-flowing and constant.

Nip disappointing behavior and responses in the bud by addressing them immediately. Don't allow your anger to simmer and boil over to the point of no return. Michelle is known to confront any issues in her relationships, friendships, and work life in a timely manner, thus reducing the opportunity for problems to grow. If, like Michelle, you've had the benefit of living with two adults involved in a loving relationship, use that stored material to your benefit by gently showing your partner the way it's done. "Gently" is the key here; he won't respond well to being beaten over the head about this or anything else. Of course one of the great things about

Barack was that he recognized his limitations on the relationship front, making it easier for Michelle to help him. Your new guy may know his limitations as well but might not be as willing to share. Following Michelle's methods in this way just may lead to success. Your guy also may not transform into the perfect man overnight, but with time and some understanding on your part he could become a more polished version of the man you'd like to grow old with.

Stay Connected

Understanding each other's needs and wants is paramount, and so is staying connected as you continue to grow individually and as a couple. While this may seem relatively easy to do early on, extra effort may be called for once the honeymoon is over, particularly if work and other demands ever call for you to have to be apart like Michelle and Barack were at various times during their relationship and marriage. Consider these ways to strengthen the bond between the two of you.

• Hang with his buddies. His friends need to see you as a real person so they won't encourage him to head in the wrong direction if some cute new face happens along. Both Michelle and Barack shared a friendship with Harvard Law professor Charles Ogletree and the three would have dinner regularly when Michelle visited Barack in Cambridge.

• When your schedules are too busy to get together, share a meal via Skype, or play a good old-fashioned board game together online.

• Take pictures of yourself and things you spot during the

day to send via your cell phone—it's the next best thing to walking down the street together.

> *Go the Extra Mile:*
> Never forget the beauty of a good old-fashioned love letter. Spritz some of your perfume on a sheet of stationery and pen your deepest thoughts to your beloved. Writing your thoughts will make you feel closer to him, and he'll have something of yours to keep.

The reason Michelle and Barack work so well as a couple is because they respect each other and they have a love built on that respect. That's the strongest love of all.

—Charles Ogletree

How to Know His Love Is Real

While women tend to have few qualms about displaying their true feelings for their mate, men oftentimes resist doing the same. As Michelle continued her relationship with Barack over the years she often wondered, as women will, if they really shared the same feelings. Barack took a calm approach to life, relationships, and love, letting things flow as they would. But beneath his cool exterior was a man who deeply loved

Michelle. It can be particularly difficult to ascertain exactly when a man falls in love with you. Contrary to popular beliefs, there are no bright fireworks at the moment it happens, but there are far more obvious ways of knowing your man cares.

It's the simple things he does that will mean everything to you. Joining you while you watch *Braxton Family Values* instead of his favorite team's game—and you're at his house. Calling or texting frequently to see how you are. Making sure your car's tires have enough air and the oil is changed. Complete support for everything you do, even if that includes attending the Bronner Bros. International Hair Show with you because your best girlfriend bailed out. That's love. As one of Michelle's childhood pastors used to preach on many Sunday mornings, "Love is a verb. It's an action word." "I love you" is great to hear but even better to feel in action. Don't forget it. Here are a few other things Michelle undoubtedly learned about men along the way and you should, too.

Men like to cuddle, kiss, and be shown attention. Besides bedroom love, most men also like to be hugged and kissed. Even the most macho of men love to be on the receiving end of an unexpected peck on the cheek or a kiss on the neck to confirm your interest in him is sincere and unwavering.

Men may actually fall in love more quickly than women. Men like to fool those around them into thinking that they're the last to develop strong feelings, but this is far from the truth. When men love, they love deeply. Though some find this difficult to believe, men can and do love as deeply as women in most cases. Once again, it's usually presented in a different fashion, making it hard for some women to recognize.

When men hurt, they hurt deeply, too. We know how it feels to hurt as women, but we need to understand men can be hurt as well. If he makes no display of sadness, we assume his feelings aren't hurt when we say or do the wrong thing. Men often suffer in silence and keep their pain private. Don't let this act fool you.

Text Like Michelle

Texting like Michelle could possibly mean not texting at all, though friends say the technology-resistant First Lady is slowly coming around to a more modern way of thinking on life and technology. The First Lady's legendary desire for privacy and face-to-face interactions would keep her from abusing this particular habit, but you may just fall victim. Still, with some forethought and common sense, your cell phone can serve its purpose, keeping the two of you as close and as connected as you desire.

Text This, Not That!

A great text life can do wonders for your busy lifestyle, and a misguided one can come back to haunt you. Here are a few ways to make the most of your texts:

Do **Text Messages That Lift the Spirit.** Just a quick line to say "Thinking of you" can cause your significant other to have the best day he's had in months. He'll remember how thoughtful you are down the road and hopefully repay you in kind.

Don't **Be Vague.** If you can't say exactly what you need to via text, wait until you can talk via phone or face-to-face to avoid miscommunication. Texting can leave a lot to the imagination and even more to misunderstanding. If what you need to convey is that important, text to ask for a good time to talk. Otherwise you may be texting apologies for a long time.

Do **Respond in a Timely Manner.** Most people have their cell phones close at hand at all times. If you wait longer than an hour to answer back to a text, some may think you're ignoring them. Text back as soon as you get a free moment.

Don't **End Anything via Text.** Texting to end a relationship of any type is bad business. Don't take the easy way out; no one deserves that.

Do **Be Creative in Your Texts.** Sending a picture of a restaurant you'd like to try with him or a funny-looking dog you know he'll appreciate lets him know that you're thinking of him.

Don't **Get Too Creative.** Never send a picture of anything you wouldn't mind being shared with the entire contents of his address book. Michelle wouldn't, and you shouldn't.

Doing the Double Dutch

Michelle thoroughly enjoyed double-dating with girlfriends, and for good reason. Double-dating instantly exposes you and your man to the inner workings of the relationships around you. You can witness up close how others handle the quirks, foibles, and issues that come along with love and life. Seeing someone else's love in action should give you the comfort of knowing you're not alone in any romantic woes you may face and may offer you an alternate perspective on how to tackle them once they arise.

Whether sharing a double date or embarking on a night that involves just the two of you, remember nothing builds romance faster than pinpointing just the right way to spend quality time with each other, while also getting that face-to-face time. Spending sufficient time together is not only fun, it's the easiest way of getting to know all the layers of your man's personality. And while it's great to spend time with friends who are in the same age range and of the same background, another smart way to learn foolproof techniques for maintaining strong relationship ties is by observing couples who are a bit older. They can offer insight in navigating the varied issues you're bound to come in contact with as you grow together, along with issues and circumstances you wouldn't have seen coming.

While spending time in Chicago during the summer of his internship, Barack became a member of Trinity United Church of Christ, which boasted a large elderly membership. Shortly after he and Michelle began to date, the two would regularly attend church services together on Sunday mornings. There they had the chance to be exposed to couples who had been married forty years and more. The church's pastor also took a special interest in Barack and Michelle during that time. He regularly invited them to his home, which allowed the couple a chance to witness his strong family ties and marriage firsthand. Surrounding yourselves with healthy reminders of what real love looks like is the surest way to keep hope and expectation alive and well in your own lives.

Rule of Thumb No. 17: Don't Forget Your Girls

In the midst of all the excitement involved with creating a new life with your man it can be surprisingly easy to neglect those people who've been your mainstays through the years. Everyone struggles with having enough hours in the day to accomplish all they have to do. When Michelle began dating Barack, not only did she have a full schedule of heavy-duty assignments from work, she was the epitome of a doting daughter, helping her mother care for her father when she could. That didn't leave a great deal of time for nights out with the girls, even if Barack was away in Boston most of the time. Still, Michelle knew she couldn't afford to isolate herself. She'd always valued her girlfriends and that wasn't going to change just because she'd met a good man.

Many women become so immersed in romance that they stop tending to other areas of their lives. If you find yourself heading down that path, stop immediately and think about those you've lost contact with over the past weeks and months. Friendships of any kind take real work to maintain. Reach out and make an effort to commit to regular lunch dates or set an exact time to receive mani/pedis with each other twice a month. Keep an updated calendar of your girlfriends' important dates such as birthdays, anniversaries, and special events. Remembering their significant moments will go a long way in reassuring your friends they remain a priority in your life. This goes double for girlfriends who are still single. Women tend to socialize with other women who share their same social setup in life. Of course this makes perfect sense, given the ease of sharing love tips, stories, and advice. But don't forget you were once single, too, and that certainly didn't limit the support or friendship you had to offer or your need to receive the same from those you love.

Unfortunately, there is a double standard when it comes to this rule and you shouldn't ignore it. If your man has only single men as friends, take note and take cover. Men can be more easily swayed into behaving similarly to the company they keep, so employ a subtle way of encouraging him to expand his horizons on the friendship front. Male friends of yours, coworkers with similar interests, or boyfriends or spouses of your girlfriends are all excellent choices to suggest he consider spending some time with.

Together but Not Always

As you arrange planned outings with friends outside of your relationship, be sure to carve out some time for you and your own personal development as well. Togetherness can be a wonderful thing but too much is just that—too much! Don't smother each other by never being out of each other's sight. A little mystery in life and in love keeps the interest intense and the fires burning. Of course Michelle and Barack didn't have the option of smothering each other at the beginning of their lives together. They spent a summer together getting to know each other before he headed back to school in another state. Even after they were married, the two were never the type to live underneath each other. They gave each other air to breathe and time to explore interests on their own. At times they spent a little more time apart than Michelle would have liked due to Barack's busy political schedule.

Use Michelle's line of thinking by continuing to pursue the interests you had before meeting your love. Michelle made the most of their time apart by spending even more quality time with her mother and gravely ill father when she wasn't at work. She'd also visit the same museums and attend the same music concerts and food festivals she normally did with Barack. Meeting the man she'd later marry didn't prevent Michelle from pursuing her own desires and dreams. Instead she continued to search for the things that would bring her happiness in both her personal and work life while fully understanding that a romantic relationship couldn't provide it all.

Being joined at the hip isn't a recipe for growth and contentment. Once you meet your dream guy, rejoice in that fact, but also make a promise to yourself to keep on track with your own life. If you've always wanted to take a ceramics class, go ahead and do it. If you usually take a yearly trip to the islands with your girls, don't stop now that you're involved with someone. The man of your dreams should complement you and your life, not halt it. Continuing to identify and develop new ideas and goals will help you remain the fascinating person he met in the first place and guarantees you won't lose yourself along the way.

It's a Family Affair

As your relationship continues pleasantly along and he successfully meets all the significant people in your life, do welcome the opportunity to do the same. There's no real need for introductions right away, particularly if his family doesn't live close or if you're still unclear on where things are heading between the two of you. Once you have a firm grasp on where things stand and where they may be going, encourage a family meeting.

Michelle had the opportunity to first meet Barack's

mother, grandparents, and half sister over the Christmas holidays in Hawaii the year after they began dating. From all accounts, the family connected immediately with Michelle, sensing her smarts and sincerity, as well as the ease Barack seemed to feel around her. Barack's sister Maya Soetoro-Ng remembers how quickly Michelle adapted to her unique environment: "From the start, Michelle was a ready convert to our lazy and fun Christmas rituals, which included Scrabble tournaments and egg-and-pancake breakfasts."

While Michelle's family's Christmases differed dramatically from Barack's, that didn't prevent the young lawyer from accepting and embracing the new world her boyfriend was introducing her to. She was well aware from the start that Barack experienced an entirely different kind of upbringing from the one she'd enjoyed, and because of that, their lives together would be a brand-new and exciting adventure much of the time. Even if you and your man have similar backgrounds, no two people are alike, so there will be differences that you can choose to fight, accept, or walk away from. Only you will know which you'll need to do.

Needless to say, one must handle the family conundrum with kid gloves because people can be incredibly shortsighted and defensive when it comes to the ones they love. His family could unfortunately be the proverbial thorn in your side, depending on how close they live to you and how much influence they have over his decisions, thoughts, and actions. Uncle Marvin with the ten kids and three wives is probably just dealing with abandonment issues according to your boyfriend's logic. Or the sister with the unpleasant attitude and a serious envy problem is really suffering from an untreated case of depression, per the family. As irritating as these traits and people may be to you, if his family is only around on holidays and special occasions, and your man exhibits a healthy way of limiting their impact on your relationship, consider them a non-factor.

Those who've met her say it's Michelle's warm and sincere embrace that draws everyone to her immediately. Her ability to relate to anyone she meets didn't develop on the campaign trail with her husband. She perfected it long before she married him. Show genuine interest in his family and give them all the benefit of the doubt. Never judge anyone; you don't know the details of their journey. Everyone can get nervous or have a bad day, so forgive his sister's bad mood and forget his father's off-color jokes. Smile, laugh, and be agreeable with everyone he introduces you to. You'll go far, just like Michelle.

Rule of Thumb No. 18: Compromise

In any relationship the ability to find a compromise will play a vital role in determining just how far you and your love will go. Barack and Michelle's friends say the pair was forced to meet each other halfway from the moment they began dating. Whether they were negotiating their work-related romance or their long-distance affair, each level they reached required a heavy meeting of the minds. Their mastery of real compromise no doubt continues to aid the Obamas in their high-profile marriage and can do the same for your budding union if you establish it early on.

The desire to compromise and sacrifice must stem from a sincere interest in the other's happiness and well-being. If you find yourself unable or unwilling to give in on even the smallest things, you may need to think a tad longer about the importance of the relationship you're in. If a true interest exists you'll find it rather satisfying to give your partner what he needs rather than resenting it. Michelle and Barack shared a genuine connection that formed at their first meeting. Key to their ability to easily recognize and respond to each other's needs was creating a clear channel of communication. Michelle's coworkers at Sidley Austin say they always noticed the couple's long and comfortable chats at the end of each workday in Michelle's office. "You'd see him sitting on the corner of her desk while she leaned in, totally engrossed in what he was saying," says one of her work peers. Having the ability to share strong and meaningful conversations on just about everything from the very beginning of your union will assist you both long-term in finding and understanding what each of you will need to last for the long haul. You certainly can't compromise on something if you don't know the what or why of it.

In their early chats Barack shared with Michelle his long-term desire to write a book about his unique childhood as a way of acknowledging his past. Years later and after they were married, Barack decided to take time off from work to write his memoir. Michelle had been aware of his goal for some time and she supported him wholeheartedly, even when work on the book took him away for extended periods of time. When Michelle decided to leave her budding law career behind, she involved Barack in every step of the process even before they were married.

Give-and-take also comes with more ease after each of you has had time to adjust and adapt to what makes the other tick. Compromising on seemingly insignificant things will have to be mastered first. Michelle loved watching old reruns of *The Dick Van Dyke Show*, while Barack preferred viewing in-depth documentaries about foreign lands and historical events. Completely different television tastes, but the two made the most of it by alternating control of the television when together and by also learning to enjoy something new on the small screen and everywhere else. "She loves dance so much, she gets Barack to watch it too," says director and actress Debbie Allen with a laugh. "She told me how she's basically turned him into a fan of modern dance and I love it. He shares her interests and her passions. What could be better than that?"

Michelle also understood full well that all fights aren't worth the trouble, and she knew the benefits and beauty of working closely with a partner over time were the trust and security it created. No relationship can survive without the ability of both partners to step back once in a while and let the other person lead. Her appreciation of the sometimes difficult and complicated art of sacrifice would truly come in handy as Barack's career began to take turns neither was prepared for. Equally as important, and another essential key to keeping things running smoothly, is recognizing when a sacrifice or compromise has gone too far. If your partner makes a request that makes you feel uncomfortable, take some time to think and ask yourself why it does. What about the request makes it impossible for you to live with? Is there another way to accomplish the same goal that the two of you can agree upon? Talk to your loved one and discuss your feelings and concerns. A strong relationship, even in its early stages, will be able to weather the storm when the two of you don't agree. Making concessions that end with regret or resentment won't bode so well for long-term love. If you feel your partner has asked for something that is unfair or unrealistic, don't hesitate to speak up and tell him exactly that.

Bond with Mama Bear

Your success in the game of compromise will surely never get tested as much as it probably will when it comes to meeting and bonding with your man's mom. If there's one family member who defies space, distance, and time, it's his mother. She may reside on a different continent and in a different time zone but she still possesses the power and influence to rock his world and yours. It can take time to discern a healthy relationship from a disturbing, codependent one. Before the untimely death of Barack's mother, Michelle was said to enjoy a warm and open relationship with her and saw her each Christmas holiday. Michelle's warmth extended to Barack's grandmother as well, who died shortly before the Obamas moved into the White House. Bonding with your beau's mom isn't always pain-free or simple, but there are steps you can take to make it a bit easier.

With any luck his mom will be likable and moderately reasonable, which should help you get along if you simply show her the respect she deserves. Kill her with kindness by complimenting her home decor, cooking, or unique accomplishments in life but keep in mind that trying too hard will only appear insincere. Make a point of asking her about her other children and extended family members as well. Let her know how much you care about her son and be sure she's aware you support him completely. If your man has his grown-up pants on, he'll already have laid some ground rules for how large his mom's presence will loom over your relationship. Ask your friends and your female counterparts in couples you respect how they developed ties with their man's mom. Desperate times call for desperate actions, so if you must, call his sister for ideas on forging a bond with their mom.

If you still sense that his mother just doesn't like you and possibly won't ever, make yourself scarce and your visits few and far between. Absence may make her heart grow fonder. Join your man in wishing her a happy birthday and a merry Christmas and in celebrating other special occasions, but leave it at that. No matter what happens in your exchanges with his mother try never to confront or argue with her about anything. No good can come from that. If marriage and kids with her son is in your future, she may have no choice but to change her perspective and approach toward you. Time may be your best friend here.

Can You See the Future?

Even when they were a thousand miles apart, Michelle felt certain she and Barack were forging a relationship that would eventually lead to marriage. Barack wasn't quite as certain. Since his mother's two marriages both ended in divorce, Barack wasn't completely sold on the notion that living happily ever after required a legal certificate. His reservations were compounded by his wish to figure out his own future before making a lifetime commitment. Michelle desired a two-car-garage, white-picket-fence existence with ample funds to live the solidly middle-class life she'd always imagined for herself.

Barack, on the other hand, had no issue with driving an old car with holes in the floor and wearing clothes that had clearly seen better days. His less-than-traditional life before Michelle had helped him avoid yearning for the trappings of upper-crust living. He'd made a decision to return to law school as an adult and that would mean living on an extremely lean income for an undetermined amount of time. Marriage hadn't been a part of his plan at that point, but meeting Michelle had turned his world around.

Sometimes it's difficult to predict where the two of you will end up as your relationship progresses. But Michelle knew what she wanted and over the course of their courtship she let Barack know as well. She didn't give him an ultimatum about marriage per se, but she did give him countless reasons to see things her way. In your journey to guide your relationship to the next level and very possibly down the aisle, carefully choose your moments to discuss what happens next. It shouldn't be an all-or-nothing conversation but more a discussion of where you'd both like to be in five years. If in your vision you clearly see you two together and he's a little less sure, a longer conversation may be in store.

Barack took the time to consider the idea of marriage for a while before Michelle kindly reminded him that she wasn't the type to wait around forever. She didn't browbeat him or attempt to play silly games. She simply made him aware of the reality he'd soon face without a commitment. He got the picture and a beautiful three-carat diamond ring was soon to follow.

Don't lose it if your guy isn't ready for marriage at the exact time you are. Listen intently and if his reasons lean toward the logical side, such as concerns about finances or job security, you'd do well to pay attention. Few relationships can stand up against the stresses of longtime job frustrations or intense money woes, particularly in the infancy of a marriage. A desire to get those basic needs in order is truly nothing to scoff at. It inadvertently points to a desire to provide the best possible life for both of you. On the other hand, if your man seems to be dragging his feet on living happily ever after for no good reason, extend the benefit of the doubt to him for only as long as it feels comfortable and then make other plans. Some of the best love affairs don't end in marriage.

Chapter Eight
Making It Work

My girls are the first thing I think about in the morning when I wake up and the last thing I think about before I go to bed.

—MO

*M*ichelle's desire for marriage, children, and a strong and stable home life echoed much of what she'd witnessed as a young child. She was in awe of her mother Marian's ability to nourish and nurture the entire Robinson family while also managing to keep her own dreams and goals in mind. As Michelle and Barack made it to the chapel in October of 1992, they began their long journey as lovers, friends, and partners in a committed union. Michelle would soon find that the landscape and rules of matrimony were vastly different from her mother's generation. Her marriage was to be anything but conventional, so she would have to develop a more modern attitude toward committed unions if her own was to thrive.

All marriages take work and Michelle's was no different. Watching her husband morph from a well-meaning lawyer and community activist to the leader of the free world was no easy chore. Still, Michelle managed it in a style that was all hers. But she didn't do it alone. She received advice and help from her doting mother and surrounding community. Michelle's entrée into marriage and motherhood wasn't without its pitfalls and detours, and yours won't be either. A good ear for listening, an appreciation for the world around you, and a genuine love between you and your husband can make a big difference in helping to mold and shape the home you want to create while learning to balance your new roles as a spouse, coworker, family member, and mother. Just like Michelle.

Settling In

As Michelle and Barack waltzed into the groove of married life, they were thankful for the support and guidance they received from those around them. Not everyone is so lucky. If you've never witnessed a healthy relationship in action, odds are you aren't completely clear on how to maintain one as an adult. Michelle had a huge advantage over Barack on this one. If you weren't fortunate enough to have your parents as relationship role models to gain wise tidbits from, you and your mate may need to look elsewhere for aid and instruction. Counseling before and during marriage can keep your love strong and your commitment to one another unwavering. While studies give the grim picture of over 50 percent of marriages ending in divorce, pre-marriage counseling is shown to decrease those odds by 30 percent. It can help you identify the behaviors and patterns that need modifying before the marriage even begins.

Counseling during marriage also reduces the rate of divorce considerably. Michelle and Barack's regular attendance at Trinity United Church of Christ and strong connection with their pastor afforded them spiritual influence and guidance for their union. You too can seek this inexpensive and often free service from your local church or parish. Many clergy are trained in marriage counseling and numerous churches offer group marriage counseling for newlyweds to share their struggles and victories with one another. Sitting together as a couple while discussing your life together long-term can do wonders for managing your expectations and taming your fears for the future, since negative attitudes and traits often don't actually rear their ugly heads until after the rice has been thrown at the wedding.

Michelle was careful not to discuss her marital issues with just anyone. A licensed therapist or clergy member is by far the best bet for you and your husband. Some men may balk at the suggestion of sharing the intimate details of your union with a complete stranger, but a few sessions could have a huge impact in creating a more serene and loving life together. Men are big on serenity. If all else fails, tell him that therapy is certainly much better than sharing those personal details with complete strangers in divorce court. That should register.

Don't Worry, Be Happy

Keeping the peace in your relationship won't always be a walk in the park, but with a little patience and forethought you may be able to reduce the tension before things get out of hand. Here are a few tricks Michelle has surely used at one time or another.

Understand that everyone's needs are different. While many women find fulfillment through loving relationships, some men find fulfillment through personal achievements and physical attention. As partners, you have to communicate your needs to each other and do your best to make sure they are satisfied.

Embrace your differences. Everyone is a product of their environment and people with varying upbringings will clash. You came from a particular way of doing things in your home and he from another. Some friction is bound to arise from this. Remember that you're combining the best from both your backgrounds to make a wonderful home of your own. In the end, it doesn't matter how the dishes get washed as long as they are washed.

Pick your battles. You may have tolerated little inconveniences or quirks like leaving the toilet seat up while dating. Once you're married, every quirky trait imaginable will be making an appearance, including the good, the bad, and the ugly. Anything that makes you uncomfortable, like his penchant for not knocking on the bathroom door before he opens it or inviting friends over for drinks without checking with you first, should be addressed immediately. After you address the issues that really work your nerves, do what you can to forget the rest. It's not worth it. Michelle famously told reporters during the 2008 campaign that Barack had stinky morning breath and often left his clothes on the floor after work. Annoying, yes; worth fighting about constantly, no.

Mind-reading doesn't apply. Communication shouldn't stop just because you are legally tied to each other. Your new husband isn't a mind reader and he can't know what you want unless you tell him. Men need clear direction on what to do to make you happy and if you don't give it, you won't be happy.

Winning isn't everything. Learning to compromise on matters both big and small is a necessity in marriage. Marriage isn't all about you and it definitely isn't about winning or keeping score. It's actually very much about sacrificing your wishes for those of someone you love, like Michelle sacrificing time with Barack to help him realize his dream of writing his memoir. If you feel that being "right" is more important than being loving toward your partner, you are in for a bumpy ride.

"I'm sorry" actually works. In order for your marriage to work, you must continue to grow as a person. Learning to admit wrongs and mistakes can be challenging, but it can also make a world of difference in mending fences and healing after a big fight. If you're not already used to using this phrase, you will be soon.

You've Got Next

Joining your lives together for better or worse can take some time to get used to. Friends say Michelle continued to sign her checks "Michelle Robinson" for nearly a year after she was married. A more serious issue you may face in the beginning stages is the question of how to actually create a healthy connection and sometimes needed distance with your loving family. Since the Obamas set up residence in Chicago after they married, they lived near many of Michelle's family members, including her mother, Marian. Mother and daughter had always shared an unbreakable bond and Michelle's marriage to Barack would do little to change that. Barack would lose his own mother shortly after the two married and that created a void Marian was happy to fill. "He embraced Michelle's mother like his own," remembers Charles Ogletree. "He loves Marian and the relationship she has with his wife. Marian welcomed him like a son and he appreciated that and still does." Barack's positive disposition toward Marian also stemmed from the fact that she'd just lost her husband, Fraser, a few years before. With the loss of his mother, he was struggling with the same type of pain. Barack had the foresight to wholeheartedly embrace his mother-in-law and in return, she offered him assistance in ways he never saw coming.

Traditionally Japanese and African-American cultures have taken pride in preserving their ties with family elders. It's considered a show of love and respect to have parents and grandparents around and involved in everyday life. "I think that's why I love Michelle so much," says Debbie Allen. "The relationship she has with her mother. I grew up with my mother's mother in our house. She was a part of all of our lives from the beginning to the end. I love that Michelle is keeping those bonds alive for herself and her children."

Aside from the historical and cultural importance of Marian Robinson's presence in the Obama marriage, she also offered Michelle a very real shoulder to cry on when problems arose in her life, work, and relationships. As Barack began to express more and more interest in entering the world of politics, it was Marian who advised Michelle to give her husband the benefit of the doubt and not complain. "She's my voice of reason on many things," Michelle says.

Michelle admits that when she raised objections to Barack's increasingly civic-minded focus and interests, it was Marian who settled her down with these words: "Leave Barack alone, he's a good man." Michelle appreciated the regular reality checks her mother freely gave and still gives and rarely questions her advice about anything. Through the years Michelle's relationship with her mother has proven as valuable to Barack as it has been for Michelle. As Barack began to travel more for his work in public office, Marian provided much-needed company and support for her daughter.

After the birth of Malia and Sasha, Marian stepped up to help Michelle take care of the girls while Barack was on the road. There's much work to be done with two young girls only a few years apart, but the idea of outsiders or nannies raising her daughters was out of the question for Michelle. Her attitude was and is that she didn't have children to pawn them off on someone else. She wanted her girls to have a childhood shaped with a similar set of values and beliefs as what she was brought up with. That couldn't and wouldn't happen with strangers in the house. Marian saw to it that her granddaughters led as normal a life as they could, particularly when Michelle began making overnight trips for her husband's presidential campaign in 2007.

With Marian in charge Barack and Michelle had no need to worry about the safety or best interest of their daughters. After Barack won the election there was no question of who'd be coming along to help the girls and Michelle adapt to their new life. Marian Robinson is the epitome of a mother who knows how and when to fit into her children's lives. She seems forever aware of where the boundaries are for her presence and opinions, always applying her wisdom layered with common sense. Marian Robinson was determined to allow her two children to make their own decisions and to follow their own path in life.

You try to get your kids not to think in the same way you did when you were coming along because you pass down—I call them "your issues," and a lot of times, they don't apply to their time and their life. They will have their own issues; they don't need mine in their head.

—Marian Robinson

As you build the life you want with your mate, make sure to include efforts that forge a positive bond between him and your immediate family. Barack knew early on how important and integral Michelle's family was to her because he'd witnessed it firsthand.

If speaking to your sister every morning is a must to get your day going, include your man in the fun too by putting him on the phone to hear her silly jokes. If your mother insists on coming over whenever she can, you may want to consider setting up weekend dinners for the family where she can be involved. Talk to your partner about it first of course, explaining, if it's the case, how much it helps to have your family around you and the benefits in it for both of you. Above all be reasonable; if your mother is seriously cramping your style or disrespecting the privacy of your home, have a discussion with her about the new rules now that you're married. Ask your entire family for help in adjusting to your marriage by giving you the room and time to figure it all out.

Mother Knows Best

The complexities of a mother-daughter relationship have been well documented over the years and without a doubt these relationships usually undergo major changes as you both get older. Whether you had a harmonious childhood or longtime contentious relationship with the woman who created you, understand that a new set of challenges will unfold once you become an adult. Michelle's relationship with her mother only got better as the years moved on, though a few disagreements between them surely occurred from time to time.

Here's a few Michelle-inspired tips to help you develop a mature relationship with your own mother and other elders.

Always show respect. You may be an adult, but you will never be on your mother's level as far as she's concerned. She may not be able to tell you what to do anymore, but you must be respectful of her thoughts and the reality that she was around long before you existed. If you do have a disagreement, make sure you express yourself in an appropriate and respectful tone.

Watch your language. Some moms are okay with vulgarity and sex talk, while others don't want to hear their offspring uttering the word "damn" in their presence. Understand your boundaries and realize your mother isn't a friend from work.

Be there. As your mother gets older she may need some of the same things she's offered you over the years. Be proactive by doing small things for her before she even asks. Take over cooking the big dinner at Christmas or Thanksgiving or order it all from Boston Market. Anything to ease her mind and workload will be appreciated for sure. If your mother is a widower like Marian Robinson, be sure to include her in as many family events as you can. Marian was present and accounted for at most Obama family events with her daughter, granddaughters, and son-in-law. Now that she resides in the White House with the First Family, she accompanies Michelle on the majority of her overseas trips, such as her 2011 trip to South Africa. The trip also included Malia and Sasha and brother Craig's older two children.

Have heart-to-hearts. There are few people who have your best interest in mind at all times. The most likely candidate is your mother. Take the time to honor the person who's had your back since birth by sitting and talking to her about the things she values and enjoys. Make sure your children do the same. They can only sense her value to them by sensing her value to you. Treating your mother with respect and kindness provides a great template for your children to follow in later years with you.

Remember that one of the most lasting lessons you can glean from your mother is how to be as wonderful a mother to your children as she was to you. Recognize the countless options and avenues you have today to learn about motherhood that your mother didn't. Just as Michelle embraced and cherished the parental blueprint Marian provided her while also adding her own personal touches, you too can build on the foundation your mother laid to get your family's future started.

Love, Marriage, and Motherhood

Michelle left her government job with the mayor's office after only eighteen months, frustrated and irritated by how slow the wheels of action actually were. Before long she'd found work as an executive director of Public Allies, an organization that trains young people for community service jobs. In the Chicago office she'd work alongside old and new friends to inspire young people from all walks of life and educational backgrounds to get involved in service-related projects aimed at helping their own communities. The job provided Michelle with the opportunity she yearned for to give back and make an impact on neighborhoods in need. But after three years another personal desire made its way to the forefront. Motherhood was always a part of the plan she had for her future with Barack.

They were married for seven years before Malia Ann arrived, but before her birth, Michelle and Barack had a nice long chat about the hopes and dreams they had for their little one. This is a must-do move before the arrival of a baby or soon afterward. Parents butt heads all the time over the way they feel their children should be raised. Be clear with each other on the vision you see for your kids as they grow. Focus on topics like schooling, discipline, and family bonding. What may appear like simple topics to begin with may not seem as simple when you take into consideration your different backgrounds and beliefs. Start the conversation now—putting it off will only make it harder.

Just the Two of You

While Michelle may have preferred an earlier appearance from her firstborn child, an extended period as a couple can be an unexpected blessing for a union. Children can turn a loving twosome into a rowdy group rather quickly and the challenges of having a new baby put a strain on many marriages. Extra time alone together can give you a chance to recognize and fix any cracks in your relationship armor while giving you an opportunity to hammer out crucial plans for your family well in advance.

No matter how strong your connection is with your mate, children are bound to change the basic dynamics of your relationship from the moment they enter the world. So savor your time as just husband and wife before babies, booties, and diapers take over.

Making the Most of Your Time Together

There is simply no love that compares to that between a parent and child. That aside, raising a child is arguably the most difficult job you'll ever have, with or without full-time help. Parenthood takes hard work, dedication, focus, and unlimited and unconditional love. So, until that time comes, experience and complete some of these other goals:

Finish school and start your career. Without a degree or steady employment, having a kid may feel like a one-way ticket to stress, poverty, and heartache. Make sure adulthood is well in hand before bringing a life dependent on you into the world.

Splurge on items that will last. When little junior arrives you'll have to cut back on a number of your spending habits to accommodate new expenses. Now would be the moment to splurge on those delicious black stiletto Christian Louboutin boots you've been pining for or to invest in that new entertainment system you've both been eyeing. Invest in timeless, well-made items that will last.

Travel abroad. Visiting distant lands and experiencing how other cultures live is an enriching experience. It can be done with children, but it is certainly easier—and cheaper—to travel without them. Do this with your mate or your girlfriends for a true bonding experience.

Explore together stateside. You don't have to go abroad to see something new. Scour the *New York Times* travel section for unique bed and breakfasts you two can visit for a quick, relaxing, and even educational weekend trip alone. Michelle's love of African-American history would have made a visit to the township of Great Barrington, Massachusetts, a must-see. The bedroom community features the former homes of historic figures like W. E. B. DuBois and James Weldon Johnson. Johnson, who penned *Lift Every Voice and Sing*, wrote many of his most famous works in a converted barn and rustic cabin that overlooks the Seekonk Brook. If you're closer to the West Coast, check into a two-day trip to Carmel, California, or Lake Tahoe, where you both can enjoy scenic views and time by the water.

Barack and Michelle's Favorite Chi-Town Restaurants

It's a not-so-well-kept secret that Michelle and Barack loved to explore and experiment with Chicago's finest eating establishments when both were in town. The Windy City is indeed a capital of culinary delights and has long offered its visitors the joys of Taste of Chicago, one of the first food festivals in the country. If you're a die-hard food lover like Michelle, plan a visit to the couple's beloved city to try a few of their favorite spots.

• The First Couple chose upscale eatery *Spiaggia* as the place to celebrate after Barack won his bid to become the forty-fourth president of the United States. The couple had celebrated many birthdays and anniversaries at this posh spot and loved it for its warm ambiance and wonderful selection of Italian dishes, paired with their equally wonderful selections of wine.

• One of Michelle's favorite weekend hangouts for date night was *Topolobampo*, gourmet chef Rick Bayless's high-end Mexican-inspired eatery, which serves up two of her favorites, tacos and black beans. "Oh, they *loved* to sit and eat slowly and talk, and I really liked that about them," Bayless recalled to *New York* magazine of their regular visits before Barack's presidency.

• Over on the west side, soul-food mecca *MacArthur's* received a mention in Barack's second book, *The Audacity of Hope*, as one of his favorite places to dine, with such delicacies as turkey legs and dressing. Obama made weekly visits to MacArthur's when living in Chicago and now makes a point of visiting each time he's in his adopted hometown.

Chapter Nine
The Challenges of Thriving and Surviving

Barack didn't pledge riches, only a life that would be interesting. On that promise he's delivered.

—MO

Michelle had a vivid vision of what her marriage should be. Though she knew it wouldn't and couldn't be an exact replica of her parents' life together she'd hoped that the unconditional love and support and pursuit of common goals she had seen in that union would also be present in the life she was now sharing with Barack. She envisioned, as many brides-to-be do, nightly family dinners filled with stories of that day's events and the daily responsibilities of the household being shared equally by husband and wife. She could foresee kissing her husband good night at the day's end, just after tucking the children in. The day after her brother, Craig, walked her down the aisle, Michelle truly believed her life with Barack would be fun, eventful, and possibly a bit daring—but ultimately quite normal. As luck would have it, the word "normal" would have no place in the life they would share.

Many women walk into marriage expecting one thing but experiencing another. The reality of matrimony and all it entails can be overwhelming and downright scary if you aren't prepared to handle the various curveballs regularly aimed in your direction. For Michelle, combined student loan debts, personal goals, and altered career directions would create quite a bit of friction in her marriage. There were no quick fixes, but she did find a way to adapt to and successfully survive the abrupt changes in her partnership's trajectory, and so can you. Pay close attention to Michelle's method of dissolving the early anger and disappointment she felt as a spouse forced to sacrifice too much. Learn how to juggle the many hats you will wear as your marriage grows deeper. Finally, discover ways to appreciate that altered or redirected dreams in your life, love, and marriage can actually lead you to a place far better than you ever imagined. Just like Michelle.

This brother is not interested in ever making a dime.
—MO on what she thought about her husband shortly after meeting him and seeing his car

---

Surviving with and Without

Much to Michelle's initial dismay Barack balked at using his newly acquired law degree to get a high-paying gig at a top-notch law firm like the one where the two of them met. Several top firms, including Sidley, offered Barack, the former president of the *Harvard Law Review*, the best spot they had available, with a nice salary to match. It didn't matter to Barack; the job he was looking for would have to include some prominent form of public service. Money meant little to the man whose first car was described by Michelle as "having so much rust that there was a rusted hole in the passenger door." Instead, Barack took a job at a small civil rights law firm and to make ends meet, he supplemented his day job with a gig teaching constitutional law at the University of Chicago.

Michelle, heavily influenced by Barack's interests and dedication to community activism, had also found work in the mayor of Chicago's office and later as a public administrator at the University of Chicago. It was a great job but sorely lacking in terms of financial rewards. Early into the marriage, Barack began to revisit his longtime desire to write a memoir about his life as a product of an African father and white mother.

Michelle offered her support to Barack, though it would mean he'd be taking on even more work in addition to the two demanding jobs he was already juggling. The couple shared their dreams, big or small, with each other, so Barack's decision to become an author came as no shock. Marriage is first and foremost about compromise on everyone's part, and that was something Michelle comprehended well, even if she didn't always like what it actually meant— in this case, more lonely nights. Still, she wanted her new husband to spread his wings and be happy in the ways he wanted most.

How are you going to afford this wonderful next stage in your life?

—MO

Rule of Thumb No. 19: Plan for Your Future

One mistake many parents make is focusing more on saving for their children's college education than their future retirement. Mellody Hobson, a friend of Michelle's and president of Ariel Investments, says this is a huge no-no. "Money can be borrowed for college educations but not for your retirement. Women and particularly people of color tend to focus on making sure their kids are able to have a better life with an education. But there are other ways of accomplishing that goal." Hobson advises her friends and family to max out the amount they can contribute to their company's 401(k) plan and to investigate opening several IRA or Roth IRA accounts. A Roth IRA is a special type of retirement account that can earn interest and be withdrawn from tax-free. Studies show that men and women are living longer lives and will require more income and savings for a longer period of time. Don't be caught off guard.

Moving on Up

When *Dreams from My Father* was republished after Barack's successful Democratic convention appearance and became a *New York Times* bestseller, Michelle had a few clear ideas on where and how the family's new financial windfall should be used. Contrary to our image of them as being on top of their financial game, Michelle and Barack wallowed in maxed-out credit cards and looming student loan debt for years. One famous story recounts Barack having his American Express card denied at a rental car company while at the Democratic convention in 2000. Their less-than-tidy finances forced the already pragmatic and cost-conscious Michelle to perfect the art of budgeting and scale back any appetite she had for the finer things in Saks Fifth Avenue.

The couple lived for more than a decade with the pressure and strain of massive student loans since both graduated from Harvard Law School. Friends estimate that their debt from student loans was in the $60,000 to $100,000 range. Barack's decision to follow a career path that offered low-paying government jobs, instead of accepting a well-paying position at a major law firm, had put a serious cramp in his family's living style. Michelle's desire to also become more civic-minded in her work didn't help their family's financial bottom line much either. Unlike Barack's low-key approach to money, Michelle hated living under the cloud of financial debt. Her desires for her family's future cost money, so it's no surprise that Barack's big payday convinced her that a brand-new reality for her family had finally arrived.

After years of work bringing the family's finances into the black, Barack received a 1.9-million-dollar advance for his next book, *The Audacity of Hope*. You and your mate may not be in line for a big cash reward, but that doesn't prevent you from developing a plan to pay off the debt you currently have. Whether the money you owe is from student loans, credit card bills, or missed car payments, becoming debt-free equals financial freedom. Discipline is one of the most crucial aspects of achieving greatness in all areas. It will help you stop increasing your debt. Decreasing the money coming out of your wallet is the only sure way of increasing your overall wealth. Keep that in mind when you see something you think you just can't live without. The purchases you make today have an impact on your financial future.

The Obamas' new lifestyle would also provide an opportunity to begin revving up their savings accounts. Saving was a practice Michelle and Barack hadn't had much time to consider as they tried to make ends meet. A comprehensive savings plan that prepares for the immediate and long-term future is necessary whether you're single or married. Having three to six months' savings available for a rainy day or unexpected job loss is still the golden rule. Arrange to have a set amount of cash automatically deducted from your paycheck each payday. This will assist you in parting with the money you've allotted to your savings. How to best use and save money should be an ongoing conversation in your family life, relationship, or marriage.

Rule of Thumb No. 20: Just Roll with It

Though Michelle and Barack discussed how to make the world a better place on many occasions before they married, she had no clue as to how and when those ideas would begin to play a pivotal role in their life together. The cause and effect of those lengthy conversations—focused on aiding those in need—would be felt shortly after the two exchanged vows. Michelle was indeed taken aback by Barack's desire to immediately pursue his personal goals instead of first building a more solid foundation for a family like she'd hoped. Though disappointed, Michelle found a way to roll with her husband's new plan and the change in the timetable she'd predetermined. Expect the unexpected. Surprises, unforeseen circumstances, and turmoil can erupt in a matter of moments, so gather your strength and handle them as best you can.

If arguments that occur in the beginning stages of marriage are not handled correctly they can also morph into resentment or irreconcilable differences as time goes on. So before blowing your cool with your partner over something you may deem important at the moment, step back, take a deep breath, and give the issue or issues proper thought and consideration.

Just a few tweaks in how you approach the beginning years of your marriage can set the tone for how you and your mate will react to disagreements or frustrations. Adopting the proper thought and response process can provide years of peace and calm down the road.

As you face some of your early disagreements, keep in mind that this is all a part of two lives coming together. Take a moment to reflect on what brought you together and how you've made it this far. Make a list to remind you of your long-term marriage goals and why this particular disagreement isn't enough to derail those plans.

Go the Extra Mile:

While Michelle and Barack were able to continue to glean bits of wisdom from the marriages of Michelle's parents and even their own pastor as they hit an early roadblock, this may be the time to revisit the premarital counseling or therapy you've already invested in or seek out the counseling you've thus far put off. The benefit of confronting whatever is causing you marital concern sooner than later can't be underestimated.

All the decisions Barack made, he made with Michelle. He'd talk to others about his goals, work, and future, but Michelle had the final say.
—Charles Ogletree

What's Next?

As Barack continued to get lost in his writing, Michelle focused on her career, which was finally inching along on the right path. She also turned her attention to another item on her list—she yearned to hear the pitter-patter of little feet in the home she and Barack shared. Pregnancy would not come quickly or easily for Michelle and at times she surely had to wonder if she and her husband were even on the same page when it came to parenthood.

As Michelle settled into her new job and pondered the wonders of motherhood and family, her husband was struggling with his own career path. Frustrated that his work with a number of public service agencies hadn't yielded major success or the results he'd hoped for, Barack found himself contemplating a move that would ultimately put considerable stress on him, Michelle, and their young marriage. After all, Michelle was just beginning to appreciate and enjoy the golfing weekends she and Barack would spend with friends like Judson Miner, the founding partner in the civil rights law firm where Barack worked, or the music festivals they'd enjoy with a host of other friends who also shared their progressive values and political interests.

"These were people who really cared about their friends and loved to spend time with them," Marilyn Katz, a longtime friend of the Obamas, explains.

Something would have to give because no longer was the future president satisfied with asking state judges to interpret the law his way. Barack wanted to actually craft the laws being implemented, and that meant running for political office. The decision to enter into the political fray seemed like a natural one for Barack, but not to his more detail-oriented, privacy-loving wife. Michelle desired a life that was in order and one she could control as much as humanly possible. Her most cherished vision was a daily routine she and Barack could put in place and maintain once their home was filled with children. Barack's intended transition into politics would put an end to those sweet dreams and any hope she harbored for living the "normal" life she yearned for. To add more fuel to the fire, a life in government would mean more time spent apart, which wouldn't exactly be helpful in her attempt to have children. How would she tackle both? Could she handle both?

Talking It Out

Much to Michelle's chagrin, Barack's burning desire to run for the Illinois senate was becoming a constant topic in the Obama household. Michelle understood her husband's need to do more but wasn't sure running for elected office was the best way to go about it. She certainly didn't fancy the idea of her husband's job taking him three hours away to the state capitol either.

Michelle hadn't planned on a long-distance marriage. The state senate convened in Springfield, Illinois, and that's where Barack would have to spend most of his time if he were to be elected. This would not be an issue the couple resolved quickly or easily.

On nights they hashed out the pros and cons of a new

direction for Barack's career, they'd often diffuse the tension by either eating out at their favorite eateries in Chicago or cooking dinner together at home. Some nights the couple would invite friends like Miner and his wife and six or seven other people over to get outside input on the ongoing debate over Barack's future.

Other nights would only include Michelle's mother, Marian. Most nights it was just the two of them, allowing ample time for soul searching and honest discussion. The couple made a commitment to each other early on in their marriage to have a date night once a week. Michelle knowingly made sure those intimate evenings usually occurred just after her Friday hair and nail appointments. Their ritual of evenings on the town once a week remained intact even after they moved to the White House.

Listen and Learn

Successful marriages require frequent and successful communication (along with great hair and nails, of course), and that can be maintained in whatever way the two of you determine works best. Take note of when discussions seem to go more smoothly. Maybe, for reasons unknown, he listens more intently just after playing his beloved Saturday morning basketball game with the guys. Or you both may listen better while sampling great food and wine, like Michelle and Barack. Invest time in figuring out when and where you bond the best.

Meeting in the Middle

Though Michelle had major reservations and much preferred to focus on becoming a mother, she gave the okay for Barack to run for the state senate. Close friends were very surprised.

No matter her reservations, Michelle proved a charming and valuable partner for her husband's political plans. Where Barack was long-winded and rambled a bit at his early fundraising events, Michelle was warm, relatable, and funny. Michelle was able to lighten up the serious tone of government with talk of travel, music, and the family they one day hoped to have. She never failed to mention her own family, who hailed from Chicago, which helped potential supporters connect Barack to the city itself.

Michelle would have her own learning curve to master, particularly in the ways political wives handled the rigors of campaigning and long separations. Despite her own impressive résumé, Michelle fought to keep whatever ego she may have had in check. No easy task for a woman accustomed to basking in the limelight of her own success story. More than getting used to her new political lifestyle, Michelle's concern was directed toward the family that was yet to come. Whereas Michelle was still holding tight to the dream of a normal existence, it was clear Barack was interested in anything but. His true fear was living an uninteresting and unfulfilled life. He didn't have to worry. He won the state senate race and was sworn in in January of 1997.

Rule of Thumb No. 21: Face Challenges Head-On

As with most things in her life, Michelle never backed down from a challenge. Any obstacle thrown at her was just another way to prove to herself and others the level of resiliency and smarts she had. When her husband's advisers spoke to her about how she could help to improve her approval ratings in any of her husband's campaigns, she did whatever it took to make those changes. This is a particularly useful trait worth developing. Dilemmas, crises, and unpleasant predicaments are part and parcel of life. You have to face them head-on, taking whatever direction or criticism may come as a result. By facing your issues immediately, you gain as much control over the situation as possible.

Baby Makes Three

A certain level of normalcy would arrive for the Obamas on July 4, 1998, when Malia Ann was born. Thankfully, the couple's first daughter arrived during the summer, when the legislature wasn't in session. Michelle, now working part-time at the University of Chicago, was on maternity leave until the fall. In *The Audacity of Hope*, Barack would write, "For three magical months the two of us fussed and fretted over our new baby." He added that while Michelle would get much-needed sleep, he would stay up with the baby until the wee hours of the morning, changing diapers, heating breast milk, and rocking his baby girl to sleep.

The arrival of fall would bring to a close the serene feeling of family life Michelle surely never wanted to end. Michelle returned to work and Barack returned to Springfield three days a week. And Michelle's mother took care of Malia while Michelle worked. At home on the weekends, many times Barack would be occupied with papers to grade from the law courses he continued to teach at the University of Chicago.

Our kids knew very early that their dad was a weekend dad. They saw him on Saturdays and Sundays.

—MO

Quality Time

By the time Sasha was born, Barack was in official political mode again, running for office. This took him away from home and Michelle, forcing the mother of two to become a single parent of sorts. This wasn't the life she thought she'd signed up for, but Michelle was in tune enough with the world around her to realize she wasn't alone in her predicament. Thousands upon thousands of women bear the daily responsibility of caring for their children with no help at all, and for reasons rarely as noble as their husbands' fighting for a better world.

It would take time for Michelle to deal with her anger over Barack's absence, but her two little girls would surely benefit from all the love, knowledge, and insight she had to offer while their father was away. Barack was in full agreement with the lessons Michelle insisted her daughters learn. She taught them the values she'd been taught and felt strongly that every child should have, such as respect for their elders and a strict work ethic when it came to school. Homework was to be completed once they returned home from school and checked by a parent before the night was done.

Michelle fiercely believed that without rules children simply go astray. She insisted that Malia and Sasha avoid video games and limit computer time during the week. Extended periods sitting in front of the television were a big no-no in the Obama household. Reading would be their entertainment escape, and Michelle regularly read them books that fed their imaginations and fueled their desire to be a part of the larger world. Malia and Sasha took piano lessons as

Michelle had also done as a child, but this time the piano was right in the family's living room. Her girls were not to miss out on any opportunity to experience something new—karate, soccer, and Girl Scouts were also part of their busy daily lives.

Carpooling with other parents was a must as Michelle juggled parenthood and work life. Marian would take up residence in the family's home for several weeks to ensure the girls arrived on time to each and every event they had, while a few of Michelle's closest friends would also pitch in to babysit or run errands.

> You do what you have to do for your children to have the lives you want them to have. It's difficult and sometimes you have no idea how you will get it all done, but you do. You may have to lean on a lot of people along the way but you'll get it done.
>
> —MO

When Barack made it home to Chicago on the weekends, the family of four took part in as many group activities as Michelle could cram into that period. Cost-conscious as ever, Michelle would search local papers and Web sites to find great deals on free community plays or cheap jazz events and festivals in the park where the children could run free. She deeply wanted her daughters to develop the same appreciation for culture and the arts that she'd embraced at an early age. She made sure the family was always in attendance when her beloved Alvin Ailey American Dance Theater company came to town and bought tickets in advance so the family's budget wouldn't be stretched even more.

Beyond "Because I Said So"

As a parent, channel your inner Michelle to help your children develop into the type of responsible and emotionally well-rounded adults you hope they will become.

Discipline them. Malia and Sasha have a strict nine P.M. bedtime. They must set their own alarms and make their beds every morning. No exceptions allowed.

Be involved. While Barack may have missed a number of Malia and Sasha's basketball games, dance recitals, and karate classes, Michelle or her mother was always there. Be present and support them in all of their interests and projects.

Work overtime. The skills Michelle learned as a lawyer at a high-powered firm also helped her develop the basics of raising smart and productive children. Think conflict resolution, communication, multitasking, time management, crisis management, and team-building.

Nurture your relationship. Watching parents interact with devotion and respect offers children a sense of comfort and security—two things they need more than anything. Michelle and Barack make a point of working well together to ensure Malia and Sasha feel protected and loved by both parents. Whether you're married with children or a single parent struggling to find middle ground with your co-parent, realize the impact you and the child's father have over your child's emotional well-being and find a way to live in peace.

Teach them to help those less fortunate. Michelle and Barack often took their children along to food banks and homeless shelters to encourage compassion and a spirit of gratitude and appreciation. Do the same by discussing the plight of the less fortunate and encouraging your children to donate toys and clothes they no longer need to other children.

Mama's Always Home

Michelle was pretty overwhelmed with the pressures of a full-time job, motherhood, and her growing frustration with a husband who wasn't around. During the week it was her job to get the girls fed, bathed, and played with in the morning. Marian stepped in to take over when her daughter's work would go into overtime. She pitched in to take the girls to doctor appointments and to playdates with other children.

Sadly, the vast majority of working mothers don't have the luxury of having a trusted family member close, ready and willing to do whatever is needed to make her life easier. Even if they do, grandmothers sometimes have other plans too. Shortly after Sasha was born, Michelle found she needed to return to work full-time so the family could stay financially afloat. Law school loans times two can take years to pay off. For one major job interview Michelle learned at the last moment that her mother wasn't available to care for Sasha. Michelle quickly moved to plan B. She simply put her infant daughter in a woven Moses basket and headed to the interview without a second thought. While Michelle did land that job with her baby girl in tow, it's best if your plan B includes an alternate caregiver whom you trust. Make a mental note of your friends' days off and call them if an unexpected situation arises, or stay on good terms with a close neighbor you wouldn't mind trusting to watch your children for a few hours if an emergency arose. If you can, and as Michelle did for as long as the family could handle it financially, work part-time so you're able to better balance mommy, wife, and job time. Depending on your line of work, take a chance and ask your employer if you can work from home a few days a week. Every little bit helps.

Continue to get in touch with your inner Michelle by discovering ways to improvise in those areas where additional assistance may be needed. Get together with your friends who also have young children and devise a plan to share daily duties like grocery shopping, dropping off your babies at day care, and sitting for one another so you each can enjoy a date night with your spouse. Even with a partner fully present and available, parenthood can be a strain on your life. Don't hesitate to reach out for the help you need.

My mother's love has always been a sustaining force for our family, and one of my greatest joys is seeing her integrity, her compassion, her intelligence reflected in my daughters.

—MO

Continuing to Fight the Good Fight

With her mother close by, Michelle managed to run the Obamas' bustling household quite successfully. As she worked feverishly to find her superwoman footing, managing the demands of home and the workplace while constantly feeling anxious about whether she was shortchanging one or the other, Barack's political career became, if possible, more complicated. He'd run for the Illinois state senate with hopes he'd be able to guide his adopted hometown toward becoming a better place for people to live, work, and raise their families. Unfortunately, as a junior senator he felt his contributions had mattered very little, so Barack announced his intent to kick his political game up a notch. He'd run for the U.S. Senate. Michelle was not amused by this and let her unhappiness be known to anyone around. A U.S. Senate post would mean Barack spending even more time away from the family home.

Barack didn't think Michelle's anger could get any worse. He was wrong. During the campaign Barack would regularly get stuck in Springfield during extended sessions. His staff would sometimes ask his wife to fill in for him at a campaign event. She was known to say no in a heartbeat.

"It was no secret among us who were helping to run his campaign that Michelle was not wild about it," says Al Kindle, a political consultant on the Senate campaign.

Barack recalled in his memoir that Michelle put up no pretense of being happy with his decision. He also recounted a tense Christmas holiday in Hawaii where Michelle barely spoke to him. Her response to the couple's serious issues probably didn't make for a merry Christmas for anyone. Strife in your life and with your mate will come and go, but it shouldn't be allowed to rain on other people's parade. Children especially aren't equipped to handle adult stress, so avoid placing them in a situation where they have to. Michelle later discovered more successful ways of getting her point across to her husband that didn't include inviting others into their personal business. If you don't want the input of others about the state of your relationship, don't put your relationship issues on blast for all to see. If the vitriol between you and your partner is that harsh, do yourself and others a favor by staying home—and use that time together to talk it out.

I see true love when I see Barack and Michelle together. Love that they've had for a while and have worked hard to keep, nurture, and have.

—Jada Pinkett Smith

Standing by Your Man When It Isn't Fun

Despite the severity of the problems she and Barack were facing, Michelle managed to have faith that her marriage could survive the damage politics was causing. It would never be easy. She was faced with a daily conundrum. At times she loved the attention, the perks, and the adulation that surrounded the world of a civil servant and his or her family. At other times Michelle despised it. Even as they entered the White House in 2008, both Michelle and Barack continued to speak about their never-ending struggle to balance family, work, and love while being fair to one another. Just like the Obamas, you too may encounter an issue or circumstance that reoccurs in your marriage. Understand that every problem you two face won't have a quick fix, so it's imperative to find ways to disagree agreeably.

Rule of Thumb No. 22: Fight Fair

Disagreements as paramount as whether or not your mate will or will not run for public office that could eventually lead to his or her becoming the leader of the free world probably won't invade your relationship very often. Nonetheless, disagreements are bound to break loose in even the strongest of marital bonds. While there's little you can do to avoid a dustup every now and then, you can do a great deal in managing how you respond to it.

Take heed if you weren't fortunate enough to grow up witnessing healthy conflict resolution. This may be the time to once again revert back to the help of a trusted therapist or church counselor in order to learn less emotional ways of managing whatever causes you stress at home. Many marriage counselors point out that if done correctly, conflict and healthy, fair fighting can strengthen your marriage. Make a point of limiting disagreements to fifteen minutes at a time, particularly if you're having a recurring argument. If you're making headway, push on by all means. If not, call a truce and schedule another time to discuss.

If there's something you're really angry about make sure to deal with it within forty-eight hours or let it go. Don't let it fester and explode into the fight of all fights. Whatever the topic of choice is, stick with it and try not to veer off into other issues. Don't bring up past disagreements when fighting, and definitely don't resort to using negative names when tempers flare. Try using "I" more than the accusatory "you" in sentences, and never raise your voice to yell or scream. Remember, you're not fighting to win a prize; you're fighting for your relationship.

Will He Stray and Can You Stop Him?

While Barack's new senate position kept him in Springfield most of the week and away from his home with Michelle in

Chicago, friends of the current First Lady say she never expressed the least bit of concern about her husband becoming involved in an outside relationship. His new job certainly offered the perfect opportunity for him to leave the proverbial front porch and explore the various options surely presented to him during his long stretches away from his wife.

No doubt, a great deal of men would have jumped at the chance to do just that. Despite Michelle's assertion that her husband had funny-looking ears and a rather large nose, women found the slender gentleman with the boyish looks quite attractive. His smarts and expanding résumé weren't too shabby either. Barack, money woes and all, was becoming a real chick magnet. Michelle still refused to give the idea of unfaithfulness any power over her thoughts. She knew allowing that concern to control her mind would spell real disaster for her marriage and her emotional well-being. She was handling enough as it was; there was no need to take on what-ifs.

A friend commented to Michelle once that she overheard a group of women discuss how they'd love to see Barack work out. Michelle merely laughed and went about her business with no reaction at all. She wouldn't entertain the notion of infidelity and obviously had enough trust in her husband to feel confident in his love and commitments. Friends add that if in fact Barack had betrayed their marriage vows, Michelle would have "simply killed him." Given her law background, that's doubtful, but Michelle had also laid down some savvy ground rules for her marriage that any woman would be wise to heed.

Lay your own ground rules while letting your husband know how seriously you take the commitment you two have made to one another. Let him know up front that you'll give him all the love and support he needs, as long as he does the same for you, so there'll be no confusion later on.

Give him good love. No, not just that kind. This has nothing to do with sex. Good love is giving him a meaningful relationship filled with genuine emotion and concern. This is a two-way street of course, but do make sure you are holding up your end of the bargain.

Make him aware of the consequences. In a general discussion about cheating, say after watching the old classic *Fatal Attraction*, you may add how incredibly hurt you'd be if he cheated on you and how your relationship would never be the same if he did. It's amazing what a few words can do to assist the male mind in understanding that actions have consequences.

Let him know he's special. Cheating isn't just about sex; many times it's tied to ego. Even the smallest compliment from you or a sincere interest in his work can go a long way in making him feel good. Men love to be appreciated—so go ahead and appreciate. And he should be doing the same for you.

You aren't going to be happy every day and a marriage isn't going to make you happy every day. When I see Barack and Michelle with each other I can tell they understand that. They figured it out a long time before some of the rest of us did. Like me. That's why I enjoy being around them. They have a real marriage that's faced real issues over time.

—Mary J. Blige

It Is All About You (Sometimes)

Michelle realized day by day that she was allowing her un-happiness with her husband's plans for the future to get the best of her and that it had the serious potential to impact the emotional health of her girls. She couldn't have that. Hostility and anger can easily morph into depression for you, and your children will no doubt feel it. Michelle wanted to provide a clear blueprint for a healthy relationship for her girls in the same way her parents had done for her. So she made some changes. Like Michelle, at a certain point you must make the commitment to find happiness wherever you can in your life and realize it won't always be as a result of your marriage or partner. You have the responsibility to make yourself happy and to understand that what makes you happy at forty may not be the same as what made you happy at twenty. Find out what fulfills you outside of your personal relationships and career. In order to properly support your partner and family, you need to also take care of yourself.

Time may be hard to secure but when family or friends offer to help out with the kids, accept! Make plans for a peaceful date with yourself, be it a ninety-minute hot-stone massage, an extended yoga lesson or an afternoon with just you and the book you've been longing to read for months. Michelle recently became addicted to the benefits and delights of antiaging massages. She received her first one on a spa trip with friends in 2010 and loved that it involved the application of various oils, such as grape, olive, and castor, that leave the skin with a soft glow and sheen. Returning to some of the simple joys that made you happy before marriage and motherhood arrived can also remind you of how far you've come and how fortunate you are to have a healthy and full life. You and your emotional well-being are essential to your family's future. Your marriage, your children, and your career have no chance of success or survival if you aren't on your A game.

Putting Your Children First

As Michelle worked to have a better attitude toward her circumstances, her priorities in life became more clear. Particularly the well-being of her children. Michelle and Barack sacrificed their already strained incomes to enroll the girls in private schools and pinched their pennies even more to secure piano, dance, and karate classes for each child. She knew she owed her two daughters all she could give them and you owe your children the same. Here's a reminder of exactly what and why that is.

Sacrifice. Children are called dependents for a reason. They need you. Whether it's the loss of sleep or driving a Honda Civic instead of a BMW so they can take tennis lessons, your children need to know you're willing to put your wants and sometimes needs aside to invest in them. Your job is to open as many doors as possible for your children so they can enjoy the best life possible.

Respect. You are the authority in your child's life, which means at no point should your children see themselves as your peers. Michelle makes a point of having fun with Malia and Sasha, but they know who the adult is in the relationship. You must teach children respect for your sake and theirs. Let them know their emotions, questions, and opinions are valid. Respect your child enough to always give them age-appropriate truth.

Discipline. Children need and really do want boundaries. Parents are responsible for providing them, so develop a system of disciplinary methods as soon as you feel they're able to understand. This will help to mold your offspring into good decision makers.

Comfort. You can never give your kids enough hugs and kisses. Your loving embrace gives them a sense of comfort and the reassurance that they are protected and valued. Take it a step further by telling your children how much you love and care for them daily.

Time. Studies suggest that children need at least thirty minutes of your undivided time each day to develop in the way they should. Driving them to school and back doesn't count. Face time means sitting down with your child to do homework or reading to your toddler. Spending quality moments with your child gives them the attention they crave and need.

Consistency. Children like what is familiar and they enjoy knowing what's coming next. Do your best to remain consistent. It can be something as simple as playing a board game as a family every Saturday or seeing a weekly movie—kids' choice—like Michelle does. Even in the midst of drama and strife, try to remain the same parent you've always been.

I spent a lot of time expecting my husband to fix things. But then I came to realize that he was there in ways he could be there. If he wasn't there, it didn't mean he wasn't a good father or didn't care. Once I was okay with that, my marriage got better.

—MO

The Beauty of an "Aha" Moment

Deciding to take charge of her own happiness, Michelle released her seething anger toward Barack and opted for a different set of tactics to tackle the situation that was robbing her of peace. Chastising Barack for his failure to be around more hadn't made a difference. The key, she decided, was to find a way to make him be more productive and involved when he actually was around. If Barack wouldn't change his lifestyle habits, she would change hers.

Without fanfare or notice, Michelle began waking before dawn to go to the gym before Barack or the girls knew she was gone. Leaving a sleeping Barack with his two daughters gave him no choice but to feed, dress, and entertain the girls while she was away. The intense workout and exercise helped her manage her hormones and emotions in a way simply ruminating over the issues hadn't, and her time away gave Barack a chance to experience what the other side of parenting looked like. Releasing her anger also allowed Barack the chance to get reintroduced to the woman he married. He hadn't fallen in love with an angry woman or a woman who couldn't appreciate the amazing life they were living. By changing her attitude Michelle ushered her marriage into a wonderful new space, a space that allowed her husband to thrive and move their lives in the history-making direction it eventually took during the 2008 presidential campaign. Michelle would reap the rewards for the years Barack wasn't home and earned the opportunity to show the world what adult love is and what it can survive.

Today, when her husband stands on a national or international stage and gazes at her with love, admiration, and trust, Michelle knows just how well deserved it is. And while she didn't initially embrace Barack's entrée into the world of politics, when she eventually got on board she became her husband's most ardent supporter. During Barack's first term in the White House, Michelle's popularity soared, as did her ability to showcase the skills she'd worked so hard to acquire and ultimately put to good use in her career, marriage, and life. Channel your inner Michelle by realizing the strength and compromise it takes to be a woman of substance and style. Your journey to empowered womanhood won't always be easy, fun, or fair, but you'll find it's worthwhile in the end. Just like Michelle did.

Chapter Ten
The House Is Definitely a Home

I'm doing what everybody does. It's just that my juggling is more public.

—MO

As with most things in her life, Michelle Obama had the basics of the kind of home atmosphere she wanted to create with Barack already etched in her mind from practically the moment they met. She cherished her childhood memories of her family home and wanted to build on that same theme of comfort and love in her own. Though the apartment she shared with her parents and brother was short on size, it overflowed with warmth, mementos of the past, and pictures of family and friends near and far.

Re-creating that world of days gone by wouldn't be easy in a new modern home, particularly since she wanted Barack's style and personality to be represented as well. As the couple's marriage grew and they moved through several different residences, Michelle found ways to incorporate both of their backgrounds and interests into the furnishings and decor of each home they purchased. She knew the environment she created with her husband would go a long way in defining and setting the tone for the life they shared and their future family. Follow Michelle's lead by taking the time to get to know what makes you and your husband tick before investing in major home purchases. Even if your partner's input is limited, make sure you keep his tastes and dislikes in mind. Decorating the bedroom in pink and lavender probably won't make him feel at home and doesn't say much for your attempt to live harmoniously. Consider how the two of you want your home to feel and what you want it to say to others.

Home Economics

Up until their marriage, Michelle's homes had only consisted of her childhood apartment, her college and law school dorm rooms, and a bungalow she shared with her mother after her father's death. Her parents' modest means meant her childhood home was clean, organized, and fully functional, but not filled with fine furniture, luxurious fabrics, and expensive art.

Friend Mattie Lawson, an interior designer in Los Angeles, says Michelle had to come into her own before truly determining her preferred choice of decorating styles.

"I think she was like a lot of young women who had to learn what they liked and didn't like in a home first. It can take a minute to find your style and you don't want to rush it by just buying anything like some people do. You have to get comfortable with you first."

This was a tough chore Michelle would face head-on when she and Barack purchased their $277,000 two-bedroom condo in a three-story walk-up near the lakefront. Michelle wasn't sure if she was up for the task of decorating the new home she and her new husband adored and purchased some months after being married. After all, she had her new job in the Chicago mayor's office to get used to and the demands of being married to a man as complex and driven as Barack to contend with.

From her own experiences, travels, and observations, Michelle embraced the universal ideal that muted and neutral colors match just about everything. She also respected the level to which both she and Barack embraced their African heritage and very much wanted that reflected throughout the home they shared. She felt strongly about highlighting the art they'd both collected over the years as well as the tribal masks and other unique pieces Barack had brought back from his travels to Africa as a young man. As a child and teen, Michelle loved viewing historic images and prints featured at the DuSable Museum of African American History in Chicago. After graduating from law school, she purchased several beloved pieces for her collection from the storied African-American museum.

Barack had little interest in the art of decorating but Michelle made sure elements of his presence and personality were felt in every corner of their home. Take a tip from Michelle and include your husband in your decoration plans even if he shows little to no interest. Trust that he is interested, just not as much as you. With just a little prodding Michelle learned rather quickly from observing her husband's reaction to different textures and styles that he loved hardwood floors, hated wallpaper of any kind, and never understood the need to paint over good, solid wood surfaces. Pay attention to your mate's comments on the decor of friends' homes or furniture pieces and art he seems to notice. Realize it's unlikely he'll fold down corners in the pages of *House Beautiful* with ideas for you to use, so sharpen your research skills and find out what you need to know in other ways.

Discover Your Home Style

If you're still trying to think of a vision for how to decorate and style your home, or just looking for some new inspiration to redesign a room or two, consider the following:

• What do you love? Look at the furniture and accent pieces you already have. Take a long look at the items you just can't part with because they each represent some element of your personal style.

• Do you have a favorite piece of art? Art is purely personal and doesn't need to be tied to need or function. Michelle and Barack's love of African art indicated an interest in more traditional-style furnishings and the use of dark, heavy woods and neutral colors.

• What is your favorite hotel to stay at? Whether you prefer staying in a cozy country bed-and-breakfast or a modern urban high-rise boutique hotel, your favorite place to stay when away from home has a clear design style that can help you find yours.

• Where would you spend all your time if you could? Where you choose to spend your vacations and what you bring back with you are great style indicators. Love Mexico and always return with the most vibrant colors of blue in your souvenirs? You'll probably love the hacienda look. Love your family vacations at the beach and have jars of seashells in your bathroom? Coastal cottage is your style.

Making Your Home Your Own

Once Michelle had a few ideas, she wasted no time putting them to use. Friends describe the couple's first home as low-key, homey, and decorated with culturally interesting yet inexpensive items. Michelle applied her pragmatic approach to most things in life, from makeup to china plates. She had no serious desire to turn into Suzie Homemaker and didn't intend on becoming overly concerned with handmade Persian rugs or perfectly arranged porcelain Lladró figurines.

The idea of draining their already small budget for home enhancement was never a consideration. Instead, she trolled flea markets, secondhand shops, and commercial stores like Pier 1 Imports and Pottery Barn for great deals. Target remains a favorite shopping spot for Michelle, as it provides an opportunity to score basic household items and other odds and ends that spruce up a home at reasonable prices. Of course she never passed up the chance to receive a sentimental hand-me-down from her family while decorating. A furniture piece she acquired and adored early in her marriage was the piano her great-aunt used to teach lessons on. Items that conjure memories are great conversation pieces.

She also perused art galleries, museums, and specialty stores that sold African art that she and Barack admired in all price ranges and for different decors. No matter your cultural background, surrounding yourself with wonderfully crafted objects that reflect it can do wonders for bringing definition, individuality, and beauty to your home.

Go the Extra Mile:
Thrift-store buys can look as good as new
with a simple paint job or by adding new and
updated upholstery. Keep this in mind when
decorating by selecting and purchasing furniture from flea markets, sample sales, or
even model-home sales.

Decorating Tips for the Bold and the Cautious

Living with your husband can present a number of challenges, including how to decorate the place you two will
share and possibly raise a family in. Space, funds, and rental
rules may determine just how you decorate your new abode.
Don't fret; setting up house can be a lot of fun when you consider the following.

Color. If your taste mirrors Michelle's and you prefer subtle
colors such as beige and white, switch it up a bit by considering the more modern combination of blue and brown when
decorating. Try a creamy cappuccino brown and a dusty
French blue for your walls. The two colors are still muted
and neutral enough to blend with most furniture. If your decor is still undecided, channel your inner Michelle by keeping
your basics neutral in color and style, then be on the hunt for
accessories that speak to you. Just one red side table or a
beautiful vase of flowers can turn a humdrum room into a
warm and beautiful haven of style and class until you figure
out what you'd like to do next.

Texture. Michelle employed the addition of texture and pattern to create inviting spaces in her home. In a neutral setting, a dark wood coffee table or large framed mirror can add richness to the room. Save the funky texture for accent pieces; all seating should be comfortable. Touch goes a long way in creating comfort. It's easy to alter a bedroom's feel with just a change of linens—use a furry throw in winter and a cotton one in summer.

Space. Michelle and Barack's first condo wasn't exactly sprawling, which worked out pretty well given the couple's lack of furniture. Michelle took her time choosing pieces and never had plans of overpopulating the layout with unneeded knickknacks. Instead she used mirrors and natural light to give the illusion of more space. If you're working with a small space, consider keeping your window coverings sheer—or opt to forgo using any at all. Light streaming in gives the impression of more open space. If you and your love enjoy entertaining, corral your furniture together and away from the walls. Floating your sofa in the middle of the room gives the illusion of more space, and seating arranged in a circle creates a conversation area. Try purchasing armless furniture for an airy and unfettered look.

Accessorize Your Home

Home accents and accessories can dress up any room, but the living room and bedroom are the easiest to update with just a few new flourishes. In the living room, eye-catching wall sculptures like sunbursts and stems of flowers are a unique alternative to traditional pictures in the den or living room. Add some graphic accent pillows to the couch and any chairs in your home to give them an instant blast of color that doesn't overpower. A new cluster of picture frames can be filled with anything from the latest family events to post-cards of places you'd like to visit, or places you have been that you'd like to bring into the theme of the room.

In the bedroom, if you love new bedding but don't have the space to house bulky comforters and quilts, consider a duvet, which you can switch out every season for a brand-new look. Time-worn furniture and accent pieces add instant character and charm to a home. An antique trunk can serve as a focal point and as a functional piece of furniture in any room. Store whatever you like inside. Fashion *and* function; Michelle would definitely approve.

Rule of Thumb No. 23: Use What You Have

Michelle's mantra in life and home decorating is often "Less is more." Your home or apartment doesn't have to be drown-ing in rugs, tables, and lamps for it to have eye-catching ap-peal. Choice pieces you love should have the opportunity to stand out and be noticed by friends, guests, and most impor-tantly you. That can't happen if every nook and cranny is filled to the brim with an array of objects. So if you've found a jaw-dropping cherrywood armoire that captures your heart, make it the focal point of your bedroom by downsizing the furniture around it. Or if your grandparents have just gifted the two of you with an antique breakfront to enhance your dining room, put it on a wall by itself so all eyes are drawn to it when guests enter the room. Beautiful furniture can speak volumes about your taste, style, and character. In-corporating your sense of style with pieces you find or are given by loved ones will go a long way in making your home a place both of you just can't wait to get back to after a long day at work.

Michelle's cautious and cost-conscious approach to decorating led her to use variations of beige and brown in her home's overall color scheme. She kept the walls beige and the majority of her accent pieces in neutral tones so as not to overwhelm the other notable pieces in the home. Those colors also complemented the framed African tribal masks Barack acquired over the years and the various batik designs and African mud and kente cloths layered in different rooms in the Obama home.

The arts are not just nice things to have or to do if there is free time or if one can afford it. Rather, paintings and poetry, music, and fashion, design, and dialogue, they all define who we are as a people and provide an account of our history for the next generation.

—MO

The Art of Life

After moving into the White House in 2008, Michelle wasted no time releasing her inner Jackie. Jackie Kennedy famously had more than a few ideas on how to bring a bit of her personal decorating style to the halls of the White House, and so did Michelle. While Jackie focused more on furnishings and draperies, Michelle leaned toward bringing more variety to the White House's art collection. Most notable are the pieces outside the Oval Office, where her husband spends his day. One striking addition was the Norman Rockwell painting

The Problem We All Live With. The painting is a re-creation of the walk six-year-old Ruby Bridges took in 1960 as she integrated William Frantz Elementary School in New Orleans. The artwork depicts an African-American little girl walking to school in a white dress, white socks, and white shoes. Her hair is in neatly braided plaits and she carries a book and a ruler. Though overshadowed by U.S. marshals, the little girl appears oblivious to the history she's making.

Michelle's taste factored heavily into the White House's request to borrow pieces like *Black Like Me No. 2*, a painting by Glenn Ligon that was inspired by a white man who darkened his skin in order to journey to the segregated South as a black man. The White House also borrowed *Booker T. Washington,* a vibrant oil painting by William H. Johnson depicting a former slave teaching a group of black students. *Emancipation* highlights an African-American man and his family awaiting the arrival of word that they're free. *Sky Light* is a work by African-American female artist Alma W. Thomas on loan from the Hirshhorn Museum in Washington, D.C., and hangs in the Obamas' private quarters along with a few paintings from Jacob Lawrence and Romare Bearden, two of the best-known and most highly regarded African-American artists of the twentieth century. Lawrence's most famous work, *Great Migration,* showcases the epic departure of African-Americans from the rural South en route to a better life in the urban North after World War I.

In whatever house Michelle calls her home she's found seamless ways of integrating aspects of her background and experiences to make it her own while also inviting others to learn about the culture, passions, and interests that shaped her life. Michelle has also used her love of the arts to arrange tributes to cultural icons who influenced her youth. She designed nights at the White House that showcased the projects and passions of artists for a variety of guests.

She paid homage to her longtime inspiration Judith Jamison with a night of dance in 2010, *The White Dance Series: A Tribute to Judith Jamison,* which highlighted the work of Jamison and showcased the talents of young dancers from across the country. "I'd been to the White House several times and under several presidents but I'd never been saluted before at the White House," says Jamison. "The fact that Michelle would do that for me says so much about her giving spirit and nature. The fact that she wanted to recognize those people who have given a great deal to the world of arts shows she knows how to use her influence and voice to get all people interested in this world of arts and its impact."

Staying true to her role of thoughtful and gracious hostess, Michelle stood for most of the program, which featured young dancers from all over the country performing Jamison's signature pieces. She spent the rest of the evening encouraging her guests to groove to the sounds and movements onstage. Even Malia and Sasha were on hand to watch their mom pay tribute to her idol. Dressed in a black and white animal-print dress by Byron Lars, Michelle gushed about her lifelong admiration for Jamison and the hope she was passing on that same love of dance to Malia and Sasha. "For years I have gone to watch Judith's company whenever and wherever I can. And I always try to bring these two little women with me because I want them to see Judith's gifts on display, because I want them to witness the grace and beauty that stirs our souls and connects us to each other like nothing else can," Michelle told the audience.

Michelle is the most delightful and charming woman who loves to give to others the attention and joy they deserve by celebrating them. Feeling her genuine support for me and my gifts in the warm and caring environment she created in the White House meant so much to me. Michelle does things from the heart and you feel that the moment you meet her.

—Stevie Wonder

Shortly after becoming First Lady in 1961, Jackie Kennedy displayed her deep appreciation for and devotion to the arts and music by inviting Spanish Catalan cellist Pablo Casals to the White House for a concert. In similar fashion, for a 2009 tribute to the masters of jazz, Michelle invited America's first family of jazz, the legendary Marsalis family of New Orleans, to perform. Led by Wynton Marsalis, the director of Jazz at Lincoln Center, the revered family of six sons and their father showcased their decades of music and talent to more than 150 music students in the Diplomatic Room of the White House. Before Michelle introduced the world-famous family to those in the room, she made her love for all art forms known to everyone in attendance: "Today's event exemplifies what I think the White House, the people's house, should be about. This is a place to honor America's past, celebrate its present, and create its future."

Michelle played dutiful hostess, ensuring all the students and attendees had clear views of the stage and ample time for questions and answers following the performance. Wearing a white pencil skirt, pink blouse, and white cardigan held together by a flower brooch, Michelle told those gathered that her grandfather was nicknamed "South Side" because he loved the musical jazz roots of the South Side of Chicago and had speakers belting out jazz in every home he owned. She added that jazz was the first form of music she was introduced to and that her grandparents played it at their home every day.

In 2011 Michelle and Barack invited the Motown Sound into the White House's East Room and gave guests that night a treat for their ears with performances by Seal, John Legend, and Sheryl Crow. Jamie Foxx headlined the night and filled the room with laughter by firing nonstop jokes and ad libs and doing dead-on impressions of past Motown legends. With her hair smoothed and pinned perfectly into a semi-beehive, reflecting the style of the Motown era, Michelle was flawless in a black L'Wren Scott jumpsuit and Cathy Waterman necklace. She wowed her guests at the standing-room-only event with tales of the love she'd had for the music and artists of Motown since childhood. She later got the crowd into the spirit of the evening by singing along with and swaying back and forth to the songs of Stevie Wonder, Marvin Gaye, and Smokey Robinson as performed by Seal, Legend, Foxx, and Crow for much of the two-hour show. At the close of evening, she embraced and chatted with guests as any good hostess would.

Take a few tips on hosting the perfect gathering from the Obamas' friend Mattie Lawson, who along with her husband, Michael, has hosted several lavish events for Barack and Michelle Obama in their fabulous thirteen-thousand-square-foot mansion in Los Angeles, formerly owned by boxing legend Muhammad Ali. Lawson says a good hostess is always mindful of her guest list when planning a party, event, or celebration.

She knows that the list is key in assembling just the right mix of personalities, locale, and energy for a night her guests will remember. Even if your list doesn't include the likes of Stevie Wonder and Sheryl Crow, you'll still want to provide your guests with good food, good conversation, and good times.

Do Your Homework

Being a fabulous host also means being well prepared, says Lawson. Stock up for unforeseen emergencies and setbacks by ordering more than what you think you may need. A great hostess always has enough food and drink to go around. Lawson suggests you keep your guests in mind when choosing a menu and offer a vast and varied selection for diverse tastes. Select music that invites a harmonious mood among your guests and keep universally loved tracks by Frank Sinatra, Marvin Gaye, and Norah Jones in your sound system to ensure the music plays all night. Michelle loved gathering a few friends in the couple's Chicago condo for a night of spicy chili, good conversation, and mellow R & B music flowing from room to room.

Share the labor. While Lawson uses her personal party planner William Miller of W. P. Miller Special Events to organize her major events, you needn't go that far. Simply enlist good friends and family to help out where needed. Be sure not to overextend yourself or you'll be too tired to enjoy your own party. Assign duties to people you can depend on to ensure that everything goes smoothly, and spend your energy on the following important aspects of being a hostess.

Set the mood. Lawson suggests that you introduce as many people as you can to one another and, to get the conversation flowing, say more than the person's name during the introduction. For example: "George, this is Patti, and she just returned from Africa a few weeks ago." That added bit of info provides an easy way for your guests to immediately connect.

Dress to impress. Michelle always looks comfortable and chic when hosting an event at either the White House or at home in Chicago. Do the same by donning the most amazing outfit in your closet, says Lawson. This is your night to shine, and since you'll be the first person your guests see when they arrive, make the view a pleasant one.

Smile, smile, and smile. Smiling is essential for all hosts, says Lawson, and that smile must remain no matter what happens as the night develops. Even if, say, a guest breaks your beloved antique lamp, never lose your cool. Just smile and clean up the mess. Any hissy fit should happen after your guests have left.

Mingle with everyone. As soon as you feel comfortable that your party's going along as planned, make a point of mingling with old and new faces. Perfect the art of small talk by leaving the controversial and hard-core topics at the office. A party is supposed to be fun, so keep the conversation light and airy. Michelle was the master of steering Barack's fundraisers away from nonstop politics with talk of family, music, and life in the big city. Follow her lead for a more enjoyable evening.

Don't forget to enjoy yourself. Lawson's last tip for being a fabulous and gracious host is to have a wonderful time at your own party. She says, "If you're not having fun, how can anyone else?"

Making Room for Family

Knowing how to host a fabulous soiree is a skill that will be useful throughout your life, but the foundation for any good house party is the home that you have created. Creating a loving and nurturing home with your partner and children is an art learned through careful practice. Just as Michelle incorporated Barack's personality into their home's scheme, she worked to do the same with her girls once they were born. To ensure they felt loved and encouraged at all times, Michelle filled the family's home with kid-friendly items. She never wanted her girls banned from certain areas of their home for fear of crayon marks and spills, so the living room couches had washable covers and most rooms had stain-resistant carpet. As you begin to build a home life you and your family can enjoy, remember you're not just choosing furniture and fabric. The home you create today will provide the backdrop for all the memories you and your family will cherish tomorrow. Make sure that each room is one that you want to spend time in as a family, bonding and creating traditions such as reading your favorite children's books together.

Top Five Books to Read with Your Kids

Michelle regularly discusses the importance of parents turning off the TV, video games, and social media to engage in meaningful conversations with their children. Sharing a story provides entertainment and keeps kids attentive, so check out one of these age-appropriate titles.

- *The Very Hungry Caterpillar* by Eric Carle (ages 0–4)

The text of this tale of a caterpillar's transformation into a butterfly isn't complex, but the message about growth and change is universal. The colorful artwork will keep your children focused on each page.

- *Where the Wild Things Are* by Maurice Sendak (ages 4–8)

Michelle loved to read this book, one of the most popular children's books, to both Malia and Sasha when they were smaller. It deals with the vivid imagination of a young boy sent to his room for being too wild. He entertains himself in a world that he's created in his own mind.

- *Green Eggs and Ham* by Dr. Seuss (ages 4–8)

You may remember being read this book as a child. It's written in the characteristically zany rhyming verse style that made Dr. Seuss one of the best-loved children's writers of all time. This book teaches one of the most important truisms of life: "If you've never tried it, you can't say you don't like it."

- *Aunt Harriet's Underground Railroad in the Sky* by Faith Ringgold (ages 4–9)

A delightful fantasy about a girl who meets Harriet Tubman on a mysterious train in the sky. Through fact and fantasy, this book takes readers on an unforgettable and educational journey.

- *Where the Sidewalk Ends* by **Shel Silverstein** (ages 9–12)

With any luck your children will enjoy *Where the Sidewalk Ends*, technically a poetry book for children, for years to come. Each poem addresses childhood concerns and presents purely fanciful stories and drawings to illustrate the author's point.

Give Them Home-Cooked Lovin'

In an effort to make sure the girls understood she was always there for them as their father's name became well-known, and to encourage free-flowing conversation with her growing girls, Michelle would often gather them both in the kitchen to make their favorite foods, like mac and cheese. Who knows, this could be the very meal over which Michelle gave Malia the dreaded "It's too soon for dating and makeup" speech. Spend quality time with your children while discovering these new recipes.

Michelle's Mac and Cheese

Serves 4

- 1 lb elbow macaroni
- 3 tbsp butter, cut into pieces
- 1 cup shredded Swiss cheese
- 1 cup grated Parmesan cheese plus 2 tbsp for topping
- 2 cups grated sharp cheddar cheese
- ⅛ tsp salt, or to taste
- 1 cup heavy cream

1 egg

¼ cup milk

Preheat oven to 350 degrees. Butter a 9 x 13–inch baking pan or casserole dish and put aside.

In a large pot of boiling water, cook macaroni until tender, 5–8 minutes. Drain in a colander and then return to the pot while still hot.

Slowly add butter, cheeses, and salt to the hot pasta, turning the noodles with a wooden spoon to spread evenly. Stir gently so as not to break the noodles.

Heat heavy cream until warm, about 30 seconds. Add egg and milk to the cream and whisk.

Stir the cream mixture into the pasta until pasta is evenly coated. Pour mixture into the baking dish. Spread evenly and sprinkle top with remaining Parmesan cheese. Bake for 30 minutes or until topping is brown.

Michelle and Barack's Favorite Chili Recipe

Serves 4

1 tbsp olive oil

1 large onion, chopped

1 green pepper, chopped

3–5 cloves garlic (to taste), chopped

1 lb ground turkey or beef

¼ tsp each ground cumin, oregano, turmeric, and basil

1 tbsp chili powder

3 tsp white-wine vinegar

2 cups chopped fresh tomatoes, or one 16 oz can
1 can red kidney beans, drained and rinsed
3 cups cooked white or brown rice
Toppings: grated sharp cheddar cheese, chopped onions,
sour cream, bottled hot sauce

Heat olive oil in a pan over medium-high heat; add onions
and green peppers and sauté until soft, 6–7 minutes. Add the
garlic and sauté a minute longer.

Add ground meat to the pan and brown, breaking it up with
a wooden spoon.

Mix the spices together with the white-wine vinegar in a
small bowl and stir into the ground meat mixture.

Add tomatoes and let simmer until the tomatoes cook down.

Add kidney beans and cook for a few more minutes.

Serve over white or brown rice. Garnish with grated cheddar
cheese, onions, sour cream, and hot sauce. Serve in sturdy
bowls over rice and with a nice, cool glass of iced tea.

Shrimp and Grits—the Obama Way

Serves 4

4 cups water
salt and pepper to taste
1 cup stone-ground regular grits
3 tbsp butter
2 cups shredded sharp cheddar cheese
1 lb shrimp, peeled and deveined

6 slices bacon, chopped

4 tsp lemon juice

2 tbsp chopped parsley

1 cup scallions, thinly sliced

1 large clove garlic, minced

Bring water to a boil. Add salt and pepper. Add grits and cook until the water is absorbed, about 20–25 minutes. Remove from heat and stir in butter and cheese.

Rinse shrimp and pat dry.

Fry the bacon in a large skillet until browned. Remove from skillet and drain well.

In remaining grease, add shrimp. Cook until shrimp turn pink. Add lemon juice, chopped bacon, parsley, scallions, and garlic. Sauté for 3 minutes.

Spoon grits into a serving bowl. Add shrimp mixture and mix well. Serve immediately.

Michelle's Favorite Baked Apples

Serves 6

1–2 tsp safflower or canola oil

6 Golden Delicious or Granny Smith apples

2 tbsp frozen orange juice concentrate, defrosted

8 tbsp dried cherries and raisins (you can substitute dried fruits like cranberries, currants, apricots, or prunes)

6 tsp honey

Preheat oven to 375 degrees.

Using a pastry brush or your clean hands, lightly coat a 6-count muffin tin with oil.

Core apples and prick tops with a fork to keep the apples from splitting while baking. Place the apples in the tin and fill each apple core with 1 tsp orange juice concentrate, 4 tsp dried fruit, and 1 tsp honey.

Bake until the apples are soft, usually 30 minutes. Serve warm.

Chapter Eleven
A First Lady's Legacy

I know that all I can do is be the best me that I can.

—MO

As in most lives and with most fairy tales, Michelle and her family's historic arrival in the White House in 2009 didn't exactly unfold as the dream come true most hoped it would be. Barack Obama and his family headed to Washington in rather dire times for the country. After defeating the odds in becoming the first African-American president of the United States, Barack Obama was immediately faced with escalating unemployment, two ongoing wars, and a huge national deficit that showed no signs of slowing down. Solutions to this myriad of problems hurting the country didn't come as easily or quickly as many believed they would, while both major political parties seemed to butt heads in ways and over issues never seen before.

Ever the survivor, Michelle graciously handled the stress

of the criticism and pressure directed at her husband, confident in Barack's ability to eventually get the country on the right track. Always the diplomat, she rarely addressed the intense scrutiny, complaints, or criticisms directly, preferring to spend her valuable energy on her girls while also focusing on developing projects and initiatives beneficial to the country's military and young children. As she steadied her focus on her future as First Lady, Michelle also ushered in a few other firsts. Interestingly and oddly enough, she was the first First Lady to bring her mother to live full-time in the White House. She also broke tradition in May of 2011 when she became the first FLOTUS to speak to cadets and their families at West Point's annual graduation family banquet held the night before commencement. She continued to add to her "first of Firsts" list when she became the only First Lady to appear on *Forbes*'s annual "World's Most Powerful Women" list.

No More Drama

Wonderfully adept at sidestepping controversies from her years of working in corporate law, Michelle faced very few of her own public relations nightmares during her husband's first term in office. Though the infamous "Shortsgate" incident brought Michelle her first bout of harsh press, she moved forward without missing a beat. Then she smoothly rode out the bulk of the stinging criticism surrounding her trip to Spain with friends in 2010. While cleverly skirting political minefields, Michelle no doubt studied the roles other First Ladies played in their husbands' administrations. She shrewdly went about crafting her own plan to make the most impact with the least amount of drama and controversy.

Unlike her predecessor Hillary Clinton, who fought a hard

but divisive war on health care early in her husband's administration (and lost), Michelle took her time, carefully choosing
the projects, programs, and crusades she'd pursue. Because
Michelle certainly had little desire to spend time and energy
away from her two young daughters on projects that didn't
speak to her fully, she opted to direct her focus to an issue that
enfolded her love for her girls with the love and dedication all
parents have for their children. Touting obesity as one of the
most serious threats against this generation of young people,
Michelle mounted a full-time war on the nation's childhood
weight epidemic with her program Let's Move!.

In the end, as First Lady, this isn't just a policy for me. This is a
passion. This is my mission. I am determined to work with folks
across this country to change the way a generation of kids thinks
about food and nutrition.

—MO

You Are What You Eat

Let's Move!, which enlisted the help of famous names and
faces such as Beyoncé and NBA star Dwyane Wade, combined comprehensive strategies for healthy eating with good
old-fashioned common sense. Wade explained the impact
that Michelle made on him and many of the children and
families he knew. "Teaching them to eat better and get fit is
such an important message and one that doesn't always come
from someone of Mrs. Obama's stature. I know what she's
doing is important to kids who've never had anyone care that
much," he explained.

The program cited many of Michelle's personal beliefs, such as the importance of walking and regular exercise in healthy living for children and adults. While many found Michelle's desire to assist young children on their path to a healthier lifestyle commendable, others deemed the First Lady's attempts to "dictate" the eating habits of Americans simply inexcusable. Unfazed by the naysayers, Michelle forged on with her mission to educate families of every income level on the best and most inexpensive ways to feed their children nutritious meals. She even encouraged fewer desserts for parents and children alike.

For anyone paying attention, Michelle offered an early indication of her future passions shortly after entering the White House. Without attaching any particular political agenda to her actions in 2009, she and a group of students from a Washington, D.C., public school planted fruits and vegetables in the new White House garden. On the South Lawn of the grounds, the fifth graders assisted the First Lady in planting spinach, salad greens, herbs, and berries, among other crops, in the garden. Many crops grown were prepared and served in the White House and others were donated to a local soup kitchen.

Michelle really redefined the role of the First Lady when she entered the White House. She made the White House more real and more relatable to the common person. There isn't one thing fake about her and people can sense that. They feel like she means what she says and if she didn't, she wouldn't say it.

—Reverend Al Sharpton

Michelle's high-profile interest in the well-being of children and their overall lifestyle prompted several well-known food chains like McDonald's, Olive Garden, and Red Lobster to begin the process of offering more diverse and healthy menu options to their customers.

Those chains, along with LongHorn Steakhouse and Bahama Breeze, agreed to cut the calories and sodium in their meals gradually by 10 percent to 20 percent over the course of ten years.

Bringing Her A-Game

Michelle put that same unrelenting effort into her support of the military and their families, which brought her that much closer and in some ways full circle to her ultimate goal of aiding those in need. Well before the election of her husband as the forty-fourth president of the United States, Michelle displayed her unwavering alliance with the families of men and women in uniform by visiting various military bases across the country and listening to their stories of separation, fear, and survival.

After Barack was elected, Michelle continued to keep the ongoing plight of military spouses and their struggles on the front page and in the spotlight. She regularly participated in USO-sponsored events and along with Dr. Jill Biden, wife of Vice President Joe Biden, began the Joining Forces initiative. Joining Forces partners with companies, nonprofit organizations, and individuals to aid families with education, employment, and health and wellness benefits. To intensify the focus, Michelle and Jill Biden traveled the country meeting with military families while also giving them support and two shoulders to lean on. Subsequently, Michelle's appearance on the popular ABC television show *Extreme Makeover: Home Edition* in 2011 was yet another stirring example of the intense passion she has for helping those in need. In that episode Michelle worked with others in the community to rebuild a home that provided shelter for female veterans in North Carolina. Laura Bush made a similar appearance on *Extreme Makeover: Home Edition* in 2005 for victims of Hurricane Katrina. The two-hour show featured the moving and personal stories of women recently returned from serving in Iraq and Afghanistan now struggling to find employment, housing, and stability of any kind for their families. The First Lady also made a point of being present at the North Carolina home when the military families moved into the updated facility.

Michelle is bringing a sense of connection and accessibility to that position that no nation has witnessed. She is a modern-day woman in the twenty-first century, allowing us to see the best of ourselves in her.

—Oprah Winfrey

Michelle's appearance on the Nickelodeon show *iCarly* in January of 2012 championing support for military families was a home run among kids. Her earlier visits to shows such as *Oprah* and *Iron Chef* to promote her passion only helped to increase her impact and influence that much more.

That influence played a large part in her delivering a truly universal message as she traveled, at times alongside her husband, around the world as First Lady. On many of those highly publicized trips, Michelle regularly met with young people, and in particular young women, away from the cameras, encouraging them to actively engage in roles that promote leadership, service, and education.

Fulfilling one of her life's dreams, to feel the earth in different parts of the Motherland, Michelle, Marian, Sasha and Malia, and Michelle's niece and nephew all traveled to South Africa and Botswana in June 2011. The trip had deep meaning for Michelle as she served as the keynote speaker at the Young African Women Leaders Forum in South Africa. Sharing the stage with fellow speaker Oprah Winfrey, Michelle offered her thoughts on the lives of families she encountered across the U.S. and abroad. "We fundamentally want the same things for ourselves and for each other," she explained. "We want our kids to be safe and grow up with some resources and to aspire to a slightly better life than ours."

The legacy and impact of Michelle's husband, Barack Obama, will take years if not decades to fully understand and ultimately judge. First Lady Michelle Obama should face no such challenge as historians continue to analyze and define her influence on culture in the twenty-first century and her place in history. Though some may characterize her early appearances on the national stage as shaky and slightly disconnected from the masses, others will laud her ability to easily flow from a relatively private existence into the high-powered world of politics in an instant and with no blueprint or handbook explaining how it should be done by a woman of color.

There's no doubt that Michelle's passion projects and fashion choices defined and impacted her overall popularity in the role of First Lady. While Barack's popularity dropped to below 50 percent at times, Michelle's numbers rarely fell below the 60 percent mark and often peaked at 70 percent.

Many close to Michelle say they were never completely sure the "real Michelle" would ever reach those high numbers, but proving herself a woman of substance, strength, and resilience, Michelle changed many of the hearts and minds of those who were unwilling to accept a true face of change.

Michelle Robinson Obama's background prepared her for the amazing life she'd one day have and shaped her into a woman unafraid of her own opinions but savvy enough to know when and where to share them. That became an essential trait during her first few years in the White House as she smoothly sidestepped the many land mines of partisan politics her husband could not avoid. The world watched a woman already comfortable in her own skin become even more so, giving women and young girls a chance to learn how to flourish in most the difficult circumstances. She never wavered in her efforts to embrace her supporters and her critics with the same easy and relatable charm. She knew she'd make mistakes along the way, so she offered few apologies when they occurred but vowed not to make them again. She didn't.

Michelle continued to master her job as a wife, daughter, and mother even in the midst of cameras and media storms. All the while she never faltered in pursuing her calling to help others, bettering the lives of military families and the health of children struggling with weight issues. Most importantly, her determination to keep her marriage strong and her daughters secure and grounded won't stop, no matter what the Obamas' next address is. And the world will keep watching.

Sources

Much has been written on the life and times of Michelle Obama and even more documentation is available on the life and history of her husband, President Barack Obama. Along with past interviews with Michelle Obama before and after she entered the White House, original interviews with her friends, family, and associates and with the First Lady's White House office and staff all contributed to the information used in this book. Books, transcripts, and articles were also used in writing this book. Here is a list of major sources.

Key Sources

Believe in the Possibility: The Words of Michelle Obama. South Portland, ME: Sellers Publishing, 2009.

Betts, Kate. *Everyday Icon: Michelle Obama and the Power of Style.* New York: Clarkson Potter, 2011.

Colbert, David. *Michelle Obama: An American Story.* Boston: Houghton Mifflin Harcourt, 2009.

Edwards, Roberta. *Michelle Obama: Mom-in-Chief.* New York: Grosset & Dunlap, 2009.

Michelle L. Obama: The First Lady and Her Family. Limited Edition Collector's Vault. Atlanta: Whitman Publishing, LLC, 2009.

Mundy, Liz. *Michelle.* New York: Simon and Schuster Paperbacks, 2008.

Obama, Michelle. *Michelle Obama in Her Own Words: Remarks and Speeches.* New York: SoHoBooks, 2010.

Tomer, Mary. *Mrs. O: The Face of Fashion Democracy.* New York: Hachette Book Group, Inc., 2009.

Periodicals

Coburn, Marcia Froelke. "High-Low Chic: Dressed Up or Down, Michelle Stands Tall as a Natural Fashion Star." *Chicago* magazine, February 2009.

Depriest, Tomika. "National Treasure." *Upscale* magazine, October 2011.

Ellis, Rosemary. "Michelle Obama at Home in the White House." *Good Housekeeping*, February 2010.

Grigoriadis, Vanessa. "Black and Blacker: The Racial Politics of the Obama Marriage." *New York* magazine, August 10, 2008.

Henneberger, Melinda. "The Obama Marriage: How Does It Work for Michelle Obama?" *Slate*, October 26, 2007.

Leonard, Tom. "Michelle Obama: America's Next First Lady." *The Telegraph* (UK), November 2008.

Northrop, Peggy. "At Home in the World." *Readers Digest*, December 2011.

Yeager, Holly. "The Heart and Mind of Michelle Obama." *O, The Oprah Magazine*, November 2007.

Acknowledgments

So many people are responsible for this book coming together and I thank them all. My wonderful agent, Steve Troha, supported my idea for *What Would Michelle Do?* from the very start and stuck with me through the entire process. I can't thank him enough. I'm so grateful that Lauren Marino of Gotham Books saw my vision and helped make it the best book it could be. Not sure what I would have done without Lauren or her terrific and always pleasant assistant, Cara Bedick. I sincerely thank Harvard professor Charles Oglethorpe for always taking time to speak with me about his two most famous students, Barack and Michelle Obama. I thank Mattie Lawson for all of her time, wisdom, and knowledge concerning the Obamas and everything in between. I'm thankful for the assistance of Deputy Press Secretary Semonti Mustapi in the First Lady's office as well as the support and advice of Kevin S. Lewis in the press office of the White House.

I'd also like to offer my sincere thanks to all who spoke to me for this project. Mellody Hobson, Robin Givhan, Tracy Reese, Judith Jamison, Samuel L. Jackson, Kerry Washington, Bethann Hardison, Dwyane Wade, Jill Scott, Mary J. Blige, Will and Jada Smith, Sidney Poitier, and Diahann Carroll.

I truly appreciate the support and patience of *Newsweek/ The Daily Beast* and editors Gabe Doppelt and Kate Aurthur during this project.

I'm thankful to friends Chrissy Murray and Nicole Childress for being my sounding boards for this project. I thank my entire family for always supporting me in any project I try. Finally, to the inspiration for this book, Michelle Robinson Obama, thank you for teaching a new generation of women the true definition of style, charm, and grace.